Total Quality Education
for the World's Best Schools

The Comprehensive Planning and Implementation Guide for School Administrators

Series Editor: Larry E. Frase.

Multiculturalism and TQE

Addressing Cultural Diversity in Schools

Ti   n

Volume 7

Multiculturalism
and TQE

Total Quality Education for the World's Best Schools

The Comprehensive Planning and Implementation Guide for School Administrators

Series Editor: **Larry E. Frase**

The authors dedicate this series to the memory of
W. Edwards Deming, 1900-1993

Multiculturalism and TQE

Addressing Cultural Diversity in Schools

Paula A. Cordeiro
Timothy G. Reagan
Linda P. Martinez

CORWIN PRESS, INC.
A Sage Publications Company
Thousand Oaks, California

For information address:

Corwin Press, Inc.
A Sage Publications Company
2455 Teller Road
Thousand Oaks, California 91320

SAGE Publications Ltd.
6 Bonhill Street
London EC2A 4PU
United Kingdom

SAGE Publications India Pvt. Ltd.
M-32 Market
Greater Kailash I
New Delhi 110 048 India

Printed in the United States of America

Library of Congress Cataloging-in-Publication Data

Cordeiro, Paula A.
    Multiculturalism and TQE : addressing cultural diversity in
schools / Paula A. Cordeiro, Timothy G. Reagan, Linda P. Martinez.
        p. cm.—(Total quality education for the world's best schools; v. 7)
    Includes bibliographical references.
    ISBN 0-8039-6107-3 (pbk: alk. paper)
    1. Multicultural education—United States. 2. Total quality
management—United States. I. Reagan, Timothy G. II. Martinez,
Linda P. III. Title.
    LC1099.3.C67 1994
    370.19'6'0973—dc20   93-42325

94 95 96 97 98 10 9 8 7 6 5 4 3 2 1

Corwin Press Production Editor: Marie Louise Penchoen

Contents

Foreword

Possibly no subject has received greater attention in the past 30 years than cultural diversity. The professional literature, news media, and professional conferences have devoted much time to this increasingly important topic. Unfortunately, much of what is known about multiculturalism is not practiced in schools or in other segments of society.

To ensure that this valuable knowledge can and will be used in schools, authors Cordeiro, Reagan, and Martinez have taken the theoretical and emotional debate to a new level. This book supplies clear and concise definitions of the many important words and phrases surrounding multiculturalism. The authors provide principals, school board members, superintendents, and parents with easy-to-use checklists for determining the degree to which the school environment and the people in it have accepted and adopted the tenets of multiculturalism and emancipation. In addition, they offer lists of questions and techniques that school administrators and teachers can use to truly end discrimination. This book expands the current mindset about the value of multiculturalism and shows how to build fully emancipated school societies.

The authors, all international consultants, share their rich experiences with multicultural education throughout the world: in Las Palmas, Spain; in Maricaibo, Venezuela; and in Pretoria, Republic of South Africa. Dr. Cordeiro is the author of numerous book chapters and articles on cultural diversity and administrative training. Dr. Reagan is the coauthor of *Becoming a Reflective Practitioner: Pedagogy, Policy, and Practice in Contemporary American Schooling* (1991), five book chapters, and more than 50 articles for refereed journals and conferences. Dr. Martinez is a highly experienced teacher, administrator, and professor in Hispanic and Native American education.

The authors are not only academic experts in all areas of cultural diversity but they have also applied their theories as school administrators. *Multiculturalism and TQE: Addressing Cultural Diversity in Schools* represents *praxis* in its purest form, combining reflection, theory, and practice into a clear and highly usable book on the complicated and sometimes misunderstood topic of multiculturalism.

This book is the only one of its kind. Using the answers it provides, practitioners can meld the multiple strengths of cultural diversity to create cultural pluralism for Total Quality Education schools.

Larry E. Frase
San Diego State University

Preface

During the 1970s and 1980s great waves of immigrants entered the United States. In absolute numbers this immigration is among the largest in this nation's history. At the same time, we have a growing number of Native Americans, African-Americans, and Hawaiian-Americans, as well as the second and third generations of immigrant groups. These cultural groups are changing the face of the United States at an unprecedented rate. As the populations of various cultural groups expand in major urban areas, an ever-increasing number of suburban and even rural school districts have culturally diverse students arriving at the schoolhouse door. As these children and their families become a part of the U.S. public schools, their unique experiences, skills, and problems pose a challenge that is having a profound impact on this nation's future.

Most school personnel have not been trained to deal with many of the issues facing children from diverse cultural backgrounds. Topics such as equity of access, language acquisition, racial tension, multicultural education, and undocumented children are but a few of the topics that need to be studied, discussed, and dealt with by thoughtful school administrators who will examine how those issues impact children. School administrators need to incorporate these multifaceted issues into their educational values and beliefs.

This book is a modest attempt to do two things. First, we provide a basic discussion of the issues that are intrinsic to cultural diversity. We attempt to tie some of these issues to the concepts inherent in Total Quality Education (TQE) and hope that this book can serve as a first step in helping the school administrator to think about cultural diversity in schools. Second, we provide ideas for self-reflection as well as questions a school administrator needs to ask as he or she focuses on staff growth and development. Although there are several books currently available on the topic of cultural diversity in schools, few of them focus on the school administrator's role in affirming diversity.

Writing a book that can offer interesting and useful insights into the administrator's role in affirming diversity in schools and relating that role to the tenets of TQE is a difficult task. A major pitfall is the simplification of complex concepts like prejudice and discrimination. Another pitfall is the danger of "list making." For example, in chapter 4 we provide a list of questions that administrators should ask themselves regarding equity for all students. We are not saying these are the only questions a thoughtful administrator would ask, but rather we present these for your reflection.

In chapters 1 and 2 Timothy Reagan discusses the nature of prejudice and discrimination and how they are manifested in society. Reagan argues that it is not possible for educators to provide equitable educational experiences for all students unless issues of diversity are considered.

In chapter 3 Paula Cordeiro describes those practices that can negatively affect student learning. Chapter 4 suggests that the administrator must play a key role in enhancing staff and curriculum development. Cordeiro argues that our schools must be culturally responsive. In chapter 5 she discusses the roles of school leaders in working with staff, students, and families to affirm cultural diversity.

In chapter 6 Linda Martinez suggests that to develop a multicultural ethos in schools there must be fundamental shifts in patterns of thinking. She argues that facing adversity requires principals to take risks and reflect on their decisions and actions.

In the final chapter Cordeiro discusses the skills needed for total quality leadership. Given the richness that diversity brings to our schools, she challenges us to live our questions rather than to constantly seek answers. Each day brings new challenges to educators; resolving to be always questioning will keep our views current.

Finally, the Planning and Troubleshooting Guide provides an index of questions and topics that confront administrators. The guide identifies the pages in the book where discussion and ideas are found.

Paula A. Cordeiro
Timothy G. Reagan
Linda P. Martinez
University of Connecticut

Acknowledgments

The authors would like to thank Lisa McPherson for her typing of this manuscript. Her attention to detail and her patience are much appreciated. A special note of appreciation goes to David O'Brien, Peter Nisbet, and Sharon Conley for reading, questioning, and editing our chapters.

About the Authors

Paula A. Cordeiro is assistant professor and program coordinator for Educational Administration in the Department of Educational Leadership at the University of Connecticut. She facilitates the department's Danforth Principal Preparation Program and teaches courses in school administration in culturally diverse settings. She has served as the head of the American School of Las Palmas, Spain; ESL (English as a Second Language) coordinator in Escuela Bella Vista in Maracaibo, Venezuela; and as a consultant to overseas American/International schools. Current research and professional interests include the development of school leaders and school administration in culturally diverse settings.

Timothy G. Reagan is associate professor and program coordinator of Educational Studies in the Department of Educational Leadership at the University of Connecticut. He has been deeply involved in multicultural education programs in both the public schools and at the university level and has published extensively on issues related to the education of cultural and linguistic minority groups both in the United States and internationally. He is the coauthor, with John Brubacher and Charles Case, of *Becoming a Reflective Educator: How to Build a Culture of Inquiry in the Schools*, also published by Corwin Press.

Linda P. Martinez holds her M.Ed. and Ed.D. from Vanderbilt University. She is a former Bureau of Indian Affairs school principal and works with the Office of Indian Education Programs, Washington, DC. Martinez is an adjunct faculty member at the College of Santa Fe in New Mexico and the University of Arizona, Tucson. She teaches creativity in leadership and multicultural education. Currently, she lives in Tucson, Arizona, and is a consultant to both business and educational organizations on leadership and diversity.

✧ 1 ✧

Understanding Cultural Diversity

The Reality of Cultural Diversity in American Education

Cultural diversity has been a fact of life for the vast majority of teachers and students in the public schools throughout American history. Indeed, one of the motivations for the establishment of the common schools in the early and mid-19th century was the need to assimilate new immigrants (initially the Irish and German immigrants, and later the immigrants from Southern and Eastern Europe) into American life, and the focus on "Americanization" continued to be an important purpose for public schooling well into the 20th century. Even in the early years of public schooling, the schools were faced with the challenge of ethnic, cultural, linguistic, and religious diversity. Today's teachers and administrators face not only the kinds of diversity experienced by educators in earlier periods, but must do so in a vastly different social and political context, in which many of the common assumptions shared by educators, parents, and politicians in earlier periods are increasingly challenged in contemporary society.

In this chapter, we will present an overview of a number of the key issues related to cultural diversity in American education, including a discussion of what the term *culture* actually means in an educational context; the competing goals and objectives for schools as cultural agencies; the historical approaches to diversity that have been manifested in educational thought and practice in this country; the current debate about "multiculturalism" in American education; and finally, the case for a culturally pluralistic approach to education and its relationship to total quality education (TQE) as an approach to school management.

What Is a "Culture"?

To talk about culture in a meaningful way, we have to first spend a little time discussing what, exactly, we mean by culture in an educational context. The word *culture* is a slippery one; it can, for example, refer to high culture, as when one says that "Jane Smith is a very cultured person." When used in this way, it implies aesthetic elements of culture, such as music, art, literature, and so on. Although the purpose of an education can indeed be argued to be concerned, at least in part, with helping students to become "cultured" individuals in this sense, this is not really what most educators have in mind when we talk about culture and cultural diversity in education. Rather, we are using the term in more or less the same way anthropologists talk about it. As Young Pai (1990) has explained,

> In general terms, culture is most commonly viewed as that pattern of knowledge, skills, behaviors, attitudes and beliefs, as well as material artifacts, produced by a human society and transmitted from one generation to another. (p. 21)

From an educational perspective, some of the more important elements of culture include those listed in Figure 1.1.

Language often plays a central role in ethnic and cultural identification; even after an ethnic community has been largely assimilated into the dominant culture, certain terms and phrases are commonly retained as markers of ethnic identity. This is the case, for instance, with the use of certain Yiddish words and phrases as a marker of Jewish identity in the United States. Sometimes, an

Language

Native language versus dominant language (English)
Linguistic style and use of registers
Nonverbal communication

Behavioral Norms

Appropriate versus inappropriate behavior/activities
Dress
Food and eating-related matters

Learning Styles

Preferred modality (auditory, visual, kinesthetic)
Cooperative versus competitive approaches to learning
Value of education/schooling

Family and Kinship Patterns

Who is related to whom?
Close versus distant relations
Familial expectations and obligations

Gender Roles

Male and female roles and expectations
Gender conflict

View of the Individual

"Rugged individualism" versus collectivism

Historical Awareness of Cultural Community

Religious/Spiritual Beliefs and Practices

Figure 1.1. Important Elements of Cultural Identity

ethnic language functions as a "language of group solidarity" to indicate members of the community and to identify outsiders. This is the way that American Sign Language functions within the deaf cultural community, for example. Further, even where a cultural group uses English, its members may use a "marked" or socially stigmatized variety of English (such as Black English or Appalachian English). Finally, it is important to note that differences in communication style can indicate cultural identity and can often bring about cultural misunderstandings.

Behaviors and behavioral norms are also important aspects of cultural identity, and they very often differ markedly from one cultural group to another in significant ways. The amount of personal space with which individuals feel most comfortable is one example of culturally specific behavioral norms, as are eye contact patterns and the extent to which physical contact between friends is appropriate (hugging, touching, etc.). The acceptability and appropriateness of such behaviors often varies considerably among different cultural groups.

It is well established in the educational literature that different children function best with different teaching and learning styles. Although differences in terms of the most effective teaching and learning style for any particular child are of course highly personal—and indeed idiosyncratic—in nature, certain kinds of learning styles appear to be more common among different cultural groups. As James Banks has commented,

> Knowledge of the characteristics of groups to which students belong, about the importance of each of these groups to them, and of the extent to which individuals have been socialized within each group will give the teacher important clues to students' behavior. (Banks & Banks, 1993, p. 15)

Family and kinship patterns are also closely associated with membership in a specific cultural community. What counts as a family, as well as what a typical family actually is, differs considerably among cultural groups, as do kinship relationships. The degree to which a particular individual is a close or distant relative is not carved in stone as a kind of universal rule; rather, such relationships vary dramatically.

Gender roles have been discussed extensively in terms of their implications for education in the United States. However, the ways in which individuals (both male and female) view their own gender, appropriate gender roles, and other individuals is determined in part by their cultural background. The cultural contribution to gender perception, and especially to gender bias, is a difficult one. As Young Pai (1990) has noted,

> For example, in recent times, a trend has been toward encouraging people to choose their own roles according to talents and abilities across the gender or sex role categories. But the traditional view of sex roles includes two distinct sets of culturally assigned characteristics to men and women. . . . Notwithstanding the fact that gender-specific characteristics are culturally assigned, the mainstream society frequently views the traits specifically linked to females as inferior to those belonging to males. (p. 34)

An area that has clear pedagogical implications is that of how different cultural groups view the individual—that is, whether the group emphasizes the importance of the individual, individual rights, and initiative (as does the dominant Anglo-American culture), or whether it stresses the group/community (as is true, for instance, of many Native American cultural groups). Many of the traditional educational practices found in contemporary American public schools rely on competition among individual students, thus presenting a serious potential for cultural conflict for many non-Anglo-American students.

Finally, where the historical awareness of a particular cultural community differs in significant ways from that of the dominant culture, there may be serious educational consequences. For instance, although generally agreeing about the factual record, many African Americans view the lessons of American history quite differently than do most Anglo-Americans (as, presumably, do Native Americans and other groups who have experienced oppression at the hands of the dominant society). Such differences

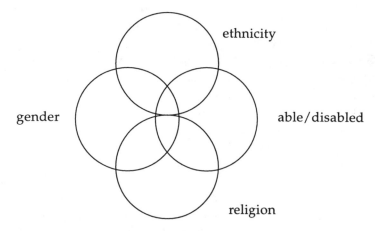

Figure 1.2. Components of Cultural Identification

in historical awareness, interpretation, and sensitivity may help to explain many ongoing debates in our society.

Finally, the religious and spiritual beliefs and practices of a cultural community often play an important role both within the community and in terms of its members' interactions with the surrounding society. Educationally, we can see the influence of such factors as the eating habits of different groups (e.g., students who eat only kosher foods, etc.), norms for what counts as acceptable attire, and issues related to specific curricular content (e.g., some Christians have objected to the use of particular novels and other materials, including *The Wizard of Oz* and other relatively common works). Religious and spiritual beliefs and practices invariably overlap other cultural issues as well, of course.

Thus far, we have spoken about culture as if it were both static and mutually exclusive in nature, but of course neither of these things is true. Cultures change and evolve over time, as a consequence both of internal developments and contacts with other cultural groups. This is why Italian Americans may be both distinct in some ways from other Americans and different from Italians (or even recent immigrants from Italy). Nor is cultural group membership always exclusive in nature; most of us actually function within a variety of different cultural groups (see Figure 1.2). In other words, one way to think about cultural diversity is that each of us is already culturally diverse, functioning in a variety of distinctive cultural spheres. As James Banks explains,

> Each individual belongs to several groups at the same time. . . . An individual may be white, Catholic, female, and middle class, all at the same time. She might have a strong identification with one of these groups and a very weak or almost nonexistent identification with another. (Banks & Banks, 1993, p. 14)

It is important to note that educators have historically viewed individuals from cultural backgrounds other than that of the dominant society in two ways: from a deficit perspective and from a difference perspective (see Figure 1.3). The deficit view of cultural difference is that differences from the cultural norm are in fact deficits that must be overcome. Thus some educators in the 1960s suggested that children who spoke Black English had a deficient knowledge of English and needed remedial or compensatory educational programs to help them overcome this deficit. Similar arguments have also been offered about other kinds of cultural differences. Although very popular in earlier years, deficit theories have been widely repudiated, and most educators today would favor instead difference theories. These merely note the presence of cultural differences and assert that, in keeping with the anthropological doctrine of cultural relativism, such differences are simply that—*differences*, about which no comparative value judgments are appropriate. It should also be noted that a deficit view of cultural diversity is incompatible, on a number of counts, with TQE. For instance, such a view would seem to repudiate such tenets of TQE as those emphasizing empowerment and vision.

Competing Models and Approaches

Given the presence of cultural diversity in any particular society, there are a number of different ways in which the society can choose to address such diversity. It is important to understand at

Deficit Perspectives	*Difference Perspectives*
The child's language is considered to be a "restricted code" of the dominant language or a less developed language than the dominant language.	The child's language is considered to be different from but comparable to the dominant language.
The child's learning style is seen as an impediment to proper academic socialization and should be adapted to culturally dominant norms.	The child's learning style is an individual matter that should be seen as a tool to help the child learn.
The child's family is often seen as "broken" or dysfunctional and as a barrier to the child's success in school.	Family patterns are understood to vary, but the child's family is seen as a key player in the child's education.
The child's behavior is problematic and the child is seen as a discipline problem.	There is often a conflict between the behavioral norms of the home culture and the school culture.

Figure 1.3. Deficit and Difference Theories in Education

this point that there is a substantial difference between cultural diversity and cultural pluralism. As the philosopher of education Richard Pratte (1979) has explained, cultural diversity refers to an empirical condition, and is basically descriptive in nature, whereas cultural pluralism is a normative claim that seeks to suggest a particular course of action. In other words, when we say that a given society is culturally diverse, all we are saying is that there are different cultural groups within that society—we are not indicating whether or not we see that as a good thing, a bad thing, a problem, or a virtue. Thus it is clear that most countries in the contemporary world are culturally diverse in nature. On the other hand, when we talk about cultural pluralism, we are asserting both the presence of diversity *and* indicating that such diversity should be valued, respected, and encouraged (see Appleton, 1983). This means, of course, that cultural pluralism is but one of several possible ways of responding to the presence of cultural diversity, as we shall see shortly, although it may be the case that a commitment to TQE also entails a commitment to some type of cultural pluralism.

Unity and Diversity: The Essential Tension

Very often, debates about cultural diversity and multiculturalism appear to posit two mutually incompatible positions about how diversity can best be addressed in American society. On the one hand, advocates of diversity focus their attention and their arguments on the advantages of cultural and linguistic diversity in an increasingly global economy, the benefits of bilingualism, and references to cultural and linguistic rights. On the other hand, advocates of a more assimilatory approach to diversity will concentrate on the advantages of a single language and dominant culture in a society, as well as on the potential for ethnic conflict in culturally diverse societies and on the history of our nation as an essentially English-speaking society.

What is missing in this two-sided debate is that both sides are, in certain ways, correct, and that both sides are, in other ways, incorrect. The mere presence of cultural diversity in a society inevitably means that there will be pressures for both cultural maintenance and cultural assimilation to a dominant norm. Very few individuals would really see functional bilingualism for individuals, even in an overwhelmingly monolingual society, as a bad thing—indeed, Anglo-Americans often see bilingualism as a valuable (albeit in our society somewhat rare) characteristic. At the same time, to function at all effectively does of course require that individuals in a common political entity must share a common core of values, including having the ability to communicate across different linguistic and cultural divides. In short, what is needed is a "middle-of-the-road" approach that takes into account both

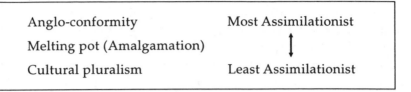

Figure 1.4. Theories of Cultural Diversity in the American Context

the legitimate rights and concerns of the dominant group in the society as well as those of other cultural and linguistic communities in the society. We turn now to a brief discussion of how Americans have tried to reconcile this tension in the past.

The American Experience in Historical Perspective

From an historical viewpoint, Americans have tried to address the challenges of cultural diversity from three distinct perspectives. These perspectives are commonly known as the theory of Anglo-conformity, the theory of the melting pot, and the theory of cultural pluralism. Each of these theories, which range from the most to the least assimilationist, will be discussed briefly (see Figure 1.4).

The theory of Anglo-conformity assumes that American society should be a linguistically and culturally unified society, held together in large part by a shared language (English) and shared cultural and political patterns. Although advocates of the theory of Anglo-conformity recognize that our society is in fact a diverse one, they believe that such diversity contains the seeds of ethnic, cultural, and religious conflict. Thus, for supporters of the theory of Anglo-conformity, the role of the school should be to "Americanize" children from different cultural and linguistic backgrounds to ensure that they are competent in English and that they identify primarily as "American" rather than as members of an ethnic community. During the late 19th and early 20th centuries, public schools in American society actively promoted this view and indeed embodied the theory of Anglo-conformity as the theoretical justification for their response to the presence of cultural and linguistic diversity. In actual school practice, the theory of Anglo-conformity was manifested in such pedagogical practices as punishing children for speaking their native language, discouraging outward signs of ethnic identity (such as clothing), and suggesting the Anglo-American cultural norm as the model for children to emulate and with which they should identify. As Donna Gollnick and Philip Chinn (1990) have argued,

> This ideology has received the most consistent support in federal policies throughout U.S. history. Through the public schools, television, and other mass communication, most children of immigrants have been thoroughly acculturated into the American macroculture, which has been influenced primarily by WASPs. (p. 19)

The theory of the melting pot, although sharing with the theory of Anglo-conformity a belief in the desirability and necessity of a single, all-embracing culture, suggests that this national culture in the American context is the result of extensive intermarriage and cultural mixing of all the different immigrant groups that have settled in the United States. The underlying idea in the theory of the melting pot is one of amalgamation—that is, that a "new race" of people is being formed in the United States and that each group has something to contribute to the "new" American character but should also identify primarily with this new hybrid. The ideal of the melting pot was actively taught in the schools as a way of assuring children that all Americans have contributed to the formation of our society. However, as Gollnick and Chinn (1990) have explained, the melting pot has been considerably more of an ideal in American history than it has been a reality:

> Although many cultural groups have made tremendous contributions to American civilization, the cultural patterns from the various groups have not melted with the patterns of the native WASPs. Instead, the specific cultural contributions of other groups have been transformed into the dominant core culture. The United States may be composed of a

number of separate melting pots. One of those may be based on religious divisions within which Whites have melted. Another may include racial groups who are not allowed to melt structurally. Still others may include certain ethic communities composed primarily of the first generation or those that choose to remain within ethnic enclaves. (p. 20)

Finally, the theory of cultural pluralism rejected the view that there should be a single, unifying culture in American society. Supporters of cultural pluralism have, since the 1960s, played an increasingly important role in changing past educational practices. The metaphor favored by many cultural pluralists is that of the "salad bowl": Just as a salad is composed of a variety of different elements (lettuce, tomato, avocado, etc.), so can a society be understood to be composed of different cultural groups that retain elements of their individual identity even while being part of the common whole. In school practice, the theory of cultural pluralism can be seen in the efforts to include people of color in textbooks, correcting past bias in terms of gender roles in textbooks, opening up the curriculum to include the contributions of women and people of color, and so on.

Although we have presented the theories of Anglo-conformity, the melting pot, and cultural pluralism as historical theories, it is important to understand that all three are still present in American education. Many teachers, administrators, and parents clearly favor an approach essentially grounded in the theory of Anglo-conformity, whereas others continue to believe in the melting pot ideal. To some extent, the success in recent years of those favoring cultural pluralism in challenging and modifying past school practices has actually intensified many people's beliefs in Anglo-conformity and the melting pot, as can be seen, for instance, in the rapid growth of the U.S. English movement, which seeks to have English declared the official language of the United States and opposes the use of languages other than English in most public settings. Nonetheless, most educators today are likely to accept views grounded in the theory of cultural pluralism, and it is from the perspective of cultural pluralism that this book is written.

Indeed, as we have already suggested, we believe that a commitment to TQE also necessarily entails a commitment to cultural pluralism.

Competing Perspectives

In contemporary American society, the challenges presented by diversity, broadly conceived, have resulted in considerable tension, debate, and disagreement among many people of good will. Many individuals and groups, both in the society at large and in its educational institutions, sincerely believe that our society is becoming increasingly fragmented as a consequence of increased attention to cultural diversity. For these people, the horrors of the former Yugoslavia, where "ethnic cleansing" and interethnic warfare and atrocities have become commonplace, provide a compelling justification for emphasizing the commonalities of the American experience. As a way of reducing or even avoiding altogether ethnic conflict, these people advocate strong efforts to promote a common core culture and language for all Americans. They believe that this is an historically "tried and true" method for assimilating newcomers to our society, and they are opposed to any sort of policy that might be taken to encourage cultural separatism.

Others, equally well-intentioned and just as committed, believe that ethnic tensions are caused not by the positive recognition and valuing of cultural differences but rather are the result of efforts to force cultural unity on dominated groups by the socially dominant group. Thus the events in the former Yugoslavia are not so much the end result of cultural pluralism as they are the result of an absence of cultural pluralism. Individuals and groups that view diversity in this way believe what is required in our society is a recognition of diversity, a toleration for differences, and a sensitivity to the legitimate concerns and values of others. This position does not, of course, actually rule out certain common values and institutions; quite the contrary—cultural pluralism, as it is generally understood today, requires the presence of a common polity and certain shared values. However, what advocates of this position do believe is that it is important not to confuse the culture of the dominant group in our society with an "ethnically neutral" set of values and norms. In other words, Anglo-American culture (that is, the macroculture) is *also* an ethnic culture.

The challenge for all of us is to imagine a society in which the rights of the individual are protected, while also ensuring that specific groups are not targeted for oppression. The problem comes when we are faced with what appears to be voluntary segregation of various sorts—women's colleges, African American social organizations, and so on. In education, the rise of what is called the "Afrocentric curriculum" is an excellent example of the tension that can arise. Is it acceptable for a school to establish a program solely for members of a particular group of students to help them succeed educationally where they might not otherwise? This is actually a very complex and difficult dilemma. On the one hand, it is clear that the public schools are disproportionately failing to educate certain groups (for instance, African American males), and such programs do seem to offer an opportunity to correct this failure. On the other hand, what such programs could all too easily become is a well-intentioned American manifestation of apartheid. As the Australian scholar Brian Bullivant (1981) has compellingly argued, social and educational programs grounded in the ideology of cultural pluralism

> are ideal methods of controlling knowledge/power, while appearing through symbolic political language to be acting solely from the best of motives in the interests of the ethnic groups themselves. (p. 291)

Further, it is important for us to keep in mind that cultural pluralism does not require that we tolerate *all* values, behaviors, and norms. For example, some cultural practices are in fact maladaptive in nature (see Pai, 1990). Others, such as sexism, racism, and so on, may be intolerable for ethical or rational reasons, and there may be good reason for us as a society (indeed, even as a culturally pluralistic society) to decide not to tolerate certain cultural manifestations that violate individual rights. As Sonia Nieto (1992) has argued,

It should be stressed that above and beyond all cultures there are human and civil rights that need to be valued and maintained by all people. These rights guarantee that all human beings are treated with dignity, respect, and equality. Sometimes the values and behaviors of a group so seriously challenge these values that we are faced with a dilemma: to reject it or to affirm the diversity it represents. If the values we as human beings hold most dear are ultimately based on extending rights rather than negating them, we must decide on the side of those more universal values. (p. 279)

This does not, however, mean that such programs are undesirable—rather, it simply emphasizes that we must be very careful indeed as we try to correct problems of the past, so as not to create even more serious problems for the future. This is, in essence, one of the central tenets of TQE: eliminate unnecessary and wasteful "rework."

The Case for Multiculturalism

Multiculturalism is the most common way in which the ideology or philosophy of cultural pluralism is put into practice in education. In this section of the chapter, we want to provide an overview of multicultural education as it is generally conceptualized, and we want to suggest that such an approach to educational practice is basically a viable and worthwhile component of good teaching.

Basically, what multiculturalism advocates is that the schools be used as agents committed to

- Promoting the strength and value of cultural diversity
- Promoting human rights and respect for those who are different from oneself
- Promoting alternative lifestyle choices for people
- Promoting social justice and equality for all people
- Promoting equity in the distribution of power and income among groups (Gollnick & Chinn, 1990, p. 31)

To achieve such an end, multicultural education must be targeted not only on children from dominated cultural communities but on *all* children, and further, it must permeate the entire school environment: curriculum, staff, student population, school organization, and so on. Another way to think about the goals and objectives of multicultural education in contemporary American society has been suggested by Young Pai (1990), who has argued that the specific aims of multicultural education include

- Cultivation of an attitude of respect for and appreciation of the worth of cultural diversity
- Promotion of the belief in the intrinsic worth of each person and an abiding interest in the well-being of the larger society
- Development of multicultural competencies to function effectively in culturally varied settings
- Facilitation of educational equity for all regardless of ethnicity, race, gender, age, or other exceptionalities (p. 110)

Much of the debate that has emerged in recent years about multiculturalism in education has had far less to do with multicultural education as it is most commonly understood and practiced than it has to do with extreme positions that are, in fact, rarely found in education. Advocates of multicultural education are overwhelmingly committed to ensuring high-quality, academically sound educational experiences for *all* children in our society. The real debate, in short, is not about quality or standards but rather about issues of justice and equity. We believe that it is simply not possible to provide equitable educational experiences for all students without taking into account issues of diversity in a positive and supportive way.

Multiculturalism and TQE

Thus far we have examined issues that are related to cultural diversity, cultural pluralism, and multiculturalism in American education. At this point, we need to change our focus slightly and direct our attention to the relationship between multiculturalism and the application of TQE in educational institutions in our society. The best way to do this, we believe, is to look at the major themes associated with TQE and see how they fit with multiculturalism and multicultural approaches to education. Marchese (1991) has identified 12 major themes of total quality management (TQM), and we will use these 12 themes as the base for our discussion of TQE.

1. *TQE focuses on quality.* The commitment to quality is central to TQE, and this commitment to quality is every bit as relevant and appropriate in educational settings as in corporate or business settings. Educational standards must be set at a high level, and students and teachers must be expected to achieve. Multiculturalism is in no way opposed to high academic standards, as has already been suggested, although it is important for us to carefully identify and justify the standards to which we will hold students. High academic standards are appropriate as long as they reflect meaningful and defensible knowledge bases that have been agreed on by the various cultural communities of which our society is composed.

2. *TQE is customer driven.* All too often in education, we forget that students and parents, as well as the society broadly conceived, are in fact our customers. It is essential that we recognize the diversity of the populations we serve and that we strive to meet their needs as effectively and efficiently as possible. To do so, of course, requires that we take into account both the diversity that characterizes our customer population and the increasingly diverse society in which all of our students will have to function.

3. *TQE emphasizes continuous improvement.* Multicultural education is based on a recognition of the limits of both our society and the individuals of which our society is composed, but it nonetheless holds before us a goal that requires continual, ongoing improvement in terms of our sensitivity to and recognition of the diversity of groups in our society.

4. *TQE concentrates on making processes work better.* Not only does multicultural education concern itself with the content of education but it also entails a serious concern with the educational process—the ways in which content is taught and learned.

5. *TQE expands the mind-set.* To take multicultural education seriously means that we focus on multicultural concerns in all aspects of the educational environment and, indeed, in all aspects of our personal lives. To the extent that multicultural education is successful, it will result in new perspectives and insights into virtually all parts of the educational process.

6. *TQE involves the discipline of information.* A variety of ongoing assessment and feedback is essential to monitor progress, both socially and individually, as we seek to make schooling a more multicultural experience. Information, not only about different groups but also about our own successes and failures in terms of meeting the needs of different groups, plays a pivotal role in effecting positive social and educational change.

7. *TQE eliminates rework.* Just as TQE seeks to eliminate unnecessary and wasteful work in the workplace, so does multicultural education seek to eliminate unnecessary, wasteful, and harmful educational practices and techniques that inhibit the development of effective multicultural learning environments.

8. *TQE emphasizes teamwork.* Multicultural education involves individuals who interact in a wide variety of different ways and contexts. An important part of multicultural education is the development of both formal and informal groups of students, teachers, and others to collaboratively work on improving the educational environment.

9. *TQE empowers people.* Empowerment is arguably the single most important purpose of multiculturalism and multicultural education. Empowerment is valuable both for intrinsic reasons and for practical and pragmatic ones.

10. *TQE invests in training and recognition.* To make a particular school or educational institution more culturally sensitive and aware, ongoing in-service training is often needed. Such training and formal recognition of the importance of multiculturalism in education can play a key role in the creation of a more tolerant environment.

11. *TQE requires vision.* Vision, in the sense of a clear, shared view of what we are trying to achieve, is essential for multicultural education reforms to succeed. The vision must be collaboratively developed and must be shared by participants.

12. *TQE requires leadership.* Related to the theme of vision, the successful implementation of multicultural education inevitably involves strong, proactive leadership on the part of school administrators. Weak or insincere support for multiculturalism not only impedes but can make impossible the development of a truly multicultural learning environment.

Key Terms and Concepts

Amalgamation. Amalgamation refers to the idea that different cultural groups in a society will interact in a variety of ways, including through intermarriage, and that the result of such interactions will be the creation of a new, common culture. In American history, amalgamation is manifested most clearly in the ideal of the melting pot.

Anglo-conformity. Anglo-conformity is the historical approach to cultural diversity in the United States that argued that our society is essentially an English-based one and that newcomers should assimilate into the dominant, English American (or Anglo-American) culture.

Assimilation. Assimilation refers to the process by which a cultural group abandons its cultural and linguistic heritage in favor of that of another cultural group. In the American context, assimilation has historically referred to the process by which immigrants have gradually, often over the course of several generations, come to adopt the dominant cultural and linguistic norms of Anglo-American society.

Culture. The term *culture,* as it is generally used by anthropologists, educators, and others, refers to the complex, changing nexus of values, attitudes, beliefs, practices, traditions, social institutions, and so on, of a community. Included as elements of culture are religion, language, foods, history, dress, and so on.

Cultural diversity. Cultural diversity refers to the presence in a particular society of different cultural groups. It is an empirical term in that it does not entail any values about the worth, or the value, of diversity.

Cultural pluralism. Cultural pluralism is used to indicate an acceptance of cultural diversity as a valuable and worthwhile facet of a society.

Cultural relativism. Cultural relativism is a doctrine that originated in the field of anthropology and that holds that it is neither possible nor desirable to evaluate or judge cultural patterns, practices, or beliefs of a community by using the standards of another community.

Deficit theory. Deficit theory refers to the idea that children (or, for that matter, adults) from another culture are in some sense "deficient" as a result of the presence of cultural differences (see difference theory).

Difference theory. Difference theory argues that cultural differences are just that—differences—and that it is not appropriate to see such differences as deficits (see deficit theory).

Macroculture. The term *macroculture* refers to the socially dominant culture in our society. This culture is also sometimes referred to as Anglo-American culture.

Melting pot. See amalgamation.

Microculture. The term *microculture* refers to nondominant cultural groups in a society.

References

Appleton, N. (1983). *Cultural pluralism in education: Theoretical foundations*. New York: Longman.

Banks, J., & Banks, C. (Eds.). (1993). *Multicultural education: Issues and perspectives*. Boston: Allyn & Bacon.

Bullivant, B. (1981). *The pluralist dilemma in education: Six case studies*. Sydney: George Allen & Unwin.

Gollnick, D., & Chinn, P. (1990). *Multicultural education in a pluralistic society* (3rd ed.). New York: Merrill.

Marchese, T. (1991). TQM reaches the academy. *AAHE Bulletin*, 44(3), 3-9.

Nieto, S. (1992). *Affirming diversity: The sociopolitical context of multicultural education*. New York: Longman.

Pai, Y. (1990). *Cultural foundations of education*. Columbus, OH: Merrill.

Pratte, R. (1979). *Pluralism in education*. Springfield, IL: Charles C Thomas.

✧ 2 ✧

Recognizing and Confronting
Prejudice and Discrimination

Understanding Prejudice and Discrimination

An important aspect of virtually every human culture has been the awareness of the difference between "us" and "them"—that is, the distinction between cultural insiders and cultural outsiders. These differences can be manifested through language, dress, religion, political beliefs, national boundaries, physical characteristics, and so on. Such differences, of course, occur both between different societies and within societies. One of the most common myths of our time is that cultural and linguistic diversity are unusual social conditions and that the social "norm" for human beings is a society in which cultural and linguistic uniformity prevails. In reality, nothing could be further from the truth. Human societies are almost always characterized by diversity, as well as by the interaction of different cultural and linguistic groups. Bi- and multilingualism, for instance, are probably far more common, both today and throughout human history, than is monolingualism. Unfortunately, prejudice and discrimination all too often have gone, and continue to go, hand in hand with diversity in human societies.

In this chapter, we will examine the nature of prejudice and discrimination, as well as some of the major manifestations of prejudice and discrimination in our own society. We will focus on racism, sexism, ageism, and other socially and personally harmful kinds of prejudice and discrimination. We will also examine the role of power relations in both maintaining and challenging such types of prejudice and discrimination, and we will discuss some of the ways in which prejudice and discrimination can be effectively challenged in the context of the American public schools. The TQE themes of empowerment, teamwork, vision, and leadership, among others, are all obviously relevant to this endeavor.

The Nature of Prejudice

Prejudice refers to a negative view of or attitude about an entire group of people. In essence, prejudice involves the prejudging of individuals based on their membership in a specific cultural, racial, ethnic, religious, linguistic, or whatever, community. Prejudice is related to, and relies heavily on, the use of stereotypes or generalizations about groups of people. We all make use of generalizations about groups in a variety of ways in our daily lives, and not all such generalizations are intrinsically harmful. Indeed, some scholars distinguish between *sociotypes,* which are accurate generalizations about social and cultural groups, and *stereotypes,* which are inaccurate or dangerous generalizations about social and cultural groups, although in general use we tend to talk about both positive and negative generalizations as stereotypes (see Bennett, 1990, p. 17). Stereotypes are not inevitably dangerous; to some extent, in fact, they are actually necessary for us to function in our increasingly complex world. As H. C. Triandis has explained,

> We stereotype because it is impossible for the human brain to employ all the information present in man's environment. Furthermore, there is a natural tendency to simplify our problems and to solve them as easily as possible. A "pet formula" such as "Mexicans are lazy" makes it possible for an Anglo employer to eliminate much of his mental effort by simply not considering Mexicans for jobs in his firm. If

he were to check on each applicant and to understand the
causes of his behavior, he would have to work much harder.
Furthermore, categorization helps perception. When some-
body tells us, "Careful, a drunken driver!" our driving
instantly becomes more defensive. The category "drunken"
implies many behaviors on the part of the other driver, and
we adjust to them quickly and usefully. (Triandis, quoted in
Bennett, 1990, p. 18)

The point is, of course, that within clear limits, certain stereotypes may be quite valuable. The problem comes in avoiding the
risk of overgeneralization of a valid general claim (e.g., drunken
drivers require more defensive driving on my part) and, even
more, of the use of stereotypes that are based on incomplete or
simply erroneous information (e.g., Mexicans are lazy). In the case
of prejudice, what occurs is that stereotyping is used not to support
clear thought but rather to replace reflection and consideration of
specific cases with preconceived biases based on ignorance. In
short, prejudice involves the inappropriate use of stereotypes.

In any given society, some individuals are likely to be very
prejudiced, whereas others are less so. Gordon Allport has studied
the development of prejudice in individuals, and his work remains the seminal psychological work on prejudice (see Allport,
1979). Allport argued that children, who begin to observe and
label certain kinds of differences among people by the age of 3 or
4, learn to categorize and stereotype (and, indeed, to overcategor-
ize and overstereotype) by late childhood and then, by adulthood,
have learned to modify their categories and to incorporate excep-
tions into their stereotypes (see Sleeter & Grant, 1988, pp. 79-81).
These stereotypes are then manifested as prejudice in those individuals who have not learned to deal with frustration effectively:

People who do not learn to handle frustration develop a
free-floating hatred that can be directed against any convenient group or individual, and that hatred can turn into
active aggression against that target. (Sleeter & Grant, 1988,
p. 81)

Interestingly, Allport's research provides intriguing support for the view that individual personality may contribute to the development of prejudice. As Sonia Nieto (1992) has noted,

> One intriguing study, for example, found a high correlation between patriotism and discrimination; that is, the more patriotic the person, the more likely that he or she would be prejudiced. This finding was explained by the fact that the person who rejects "out-groups" is more likely to have a narrowly defined idea of the "national in-group." This is the person who perceives menaces on all sides, feeling that all newcomers or those who are different from the mainstream pose a threat to an idealized and more secure past. The "prejudiced personality" is also more likely to be indiscriminate in negative attitudes and behaviors toward others; anybody perceived as "different," whether through race, religion, or lifestyle, may be the object of this person's wrath. (p. 23)

Prejudice is often talked about as if it were entirely an individual matter, but this is in fact not really the case. In fact, prejudice is not merely a matter of psychology but also exists in, is derived from, and provides support for a wide range of social, cultural, political, and economic forces (see Nieto, 1992, p. 23). Further, although prejudice has to do with *attitudes*, it is primarily of interest to us because of its implications for *action* and *behavior*. With this in mind, we turn now to a discussion of the nature of discrimination.

The Nature of Discrimination

Prejudice and discrimination are closely related concepts, but, as suggested above, whereas prejudice is concerned with attitudes and beliefs, discrimination is concerned with action and behavior (see Figure 2.1). Discrimination basically refers to the process of differentiating individuals or groups and thus is not intrinsically

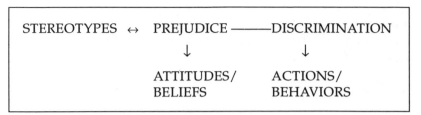

Figure 2.1. The Complex Relationship Among Stereotypes, Prejudice, and Discrimination

a bad thing. Teachers engage in discrimination whenever they grade students; the decision that one essay is better than another, or that one student has spelled more words correctly on a spelling test than another, is in fact an act of discrimination. Similarly, when a physician makes a determination about how to treat a certain set of symptoms, she is using professional judgments that are, in a fundamental sense, discriminations. Discriminations of these types are, of course, not only acceptable but are required by professional competence. The problem arises when discrimination takes place not on the basis of relevant evidence (such as medical symptoms, evaluation criteria, etc.) but rather as a result or consequence of prejudice or irrelevant criteria and evidence. In other words, when we talk about the problems of discrimination in education and society, what we actually mean are the problems associated with inappropriate kinds of discrimination. Included here would be instances of discrimination based on gender, race, ethnicity, language, sexual orientation, and so on, *where these are not appropriate criteria*. There are, of course, instances in which the use of each of these criteria might be appropriate. For example, it would be inappropriate to exclude females from a medical study of heart disease, but it would be just as inappropriate to include them in a study of testicular cancer. The issue, then, is not whether particular groups of individuals are included or excluded but rather whether their inclusion or exclusion is a reasonable and appropriate one. The same applies, of course, in educational practice.

- Curriculum
- Teaching materials
- Teaching/learning styles
- Evaluation
- Teacher expectations

Figure 2.2. Manifestations of Discrimination in the School

Inappropriate discrimination is often tied closely to personal and social prejudice. In educational settings, discrimination and discriminatory behaviors have been shown to play an important role in perpetuating the problems faced by members of minority groups, females, and others. Specifically, discriminatory behavior in educational settings affects the curriculum, teaching materials, teaching and learning styles, evaluation, and, perhaps most significantly, often teacher expectations (see Figure 2.2). A few words about how inappropriate discrimination is manifested in each of these areas may be useful.

Discrimination in the Curriculum

In recent years, there have been numerous challenges to the content of the traditional curriculum in American public schools. Many multicultural educators have argued that important elements of the curriculum remain discriminatory and inaccurate with respect to the role of women and people of color in our society. This is true especially in areas such as social studies, but it also affects other curricular areas. Although many curricular units do contain material about women and people of color, for the most part such material is included as an "add-on" rather than incorporated as an important part of the American story. This is clear, for example, in the notion of having a "Black History Month." The rise of the Afrocentric movement in American education is an attempt (to be sure, a very controversial attempt) to challenge and address this problem.

Discrimination in Teaching Materials

Textbooks and other teaching materials continue to send a variety of messages about culture, language, race, ethnicity, and gender to students. Although efforts have been made since the 1960s to correct for the inclusion of bias in textbooks, much remains to be done. Perhaps the most important element in addressing the presence of discrimination in teaching materials is the role of the classroom teacher, who must be sensitive to racial, ethnic, and gender bias in teaching materials.

Discrimination in Teaching and Learning Styles

The idea that different students are more comfortable with, and therefore are more likely to benefit from, different kinds of teaching and learning styles is hardly news for most educators, but often we forget that such preferences are related to demographic variables. This is not, of course, to argue that there is a particular "African American" or "Native American" learning style; claims about how all students in a particular ethnic, cultural, racial, or gender group will best learn are obviously invalid. Having said this, it is nonetheless also true that, as a result of socialization, members of certain groups will be more likely to benefit from some teaching and learning styles than they will from others. A classic example of this is the preference among many Native Americans for cooperative, as opposed to competitive, learning situations. It is important for the classroom teacher to be aware of such group tendencies but also to view each child as a unique individual.

Discrimination in Evaluation

Evaluation plays an important role in schooling, both in terms of its formative role and its summative role. Evaluation instruments should be sensitive to cultural differences so that they accurately measure what it is that they purport to measure. The problem of test bias, especially as it relates to children from historically dominated cultural backgrounds, has been extensively discussed in recent years, and it is essential that educators understand the limits of our evaluation instruments.

Discrimination in Teacher Expectations

Finally, it has been well established that teacher expectations significantly affect student learning. Where the classroom teacher believes that girls are not good at math, girls are considerably less likely to be good at it. Thus teacher bias and prejudice is subtly (and sometimes not so subtly) communicated to students, who often respond in the manner expected. On the other hand, as the case of Jaime Escalante, the highly successful math teacher in East Los Angeles, demonstrates, when faced with high teacher expectations, students can indeed succeed.

Prejudice and discrimination share a common origin and interact with each other in a number of ways. We turn now to a discussion of the interrelationship between prejudice and discrimination.

The Interrelationship of Prejudice and Discrimination

In seeking to respond to the educational problems presented by prejudice and discrimination, it is important to understand that both prejudice and discrimination arise out of a combination of a number of factors. These factors include the following:

- A lack of understanding of the history, experiences, values, and perceptions of ethnic groups other than one's own
- Stereotyping the members of an ethnic group without consideration of individual differences within the group
- Judging other ethnic groups according to the standards and values of one's own group
- Assigning negative attributes to members of other ethnic groups
- Evaluating the qualities and experiences of other groups as inferior to one's own (Gollnick & Chinn, 1990, p. 89)

	Discriminates	Does not Discriminate
Prejudiced	The antiminority, discriminating teacher	The antiminority, nondiscriminating teacher
Not prejudiced	The prominority, discriminating teacher	The prominority, nondiscriminating teacher

Figure 2.3. Prejudice and Discrimination: Interaction Matrix

Furthermore, prejudice and discrimination are interrelated in a somewhat complex manner, as is indicated in Figure 2.3 (see Garcia, 1982, pp. 89-91). Basically, Figure 2.3 allows us to classify teachers as falling into one of four possible categories with respect to the issues of prejudice and discrimination:

- Type 1: The prominority, nondiscriminating teacher
- Type 2: The prominority, discriminating teacher
- Type 3: The antiminority, nondiscriminating teacher
- Type 4: The antiminority, discriminating teacher

It is possible for prejudice and discrimination to exist independently of each other, as the figure suggests, because there are different kinds of discrimination. Specifically, we generally distinguish between individual discrimination and institutional discrimination. Individual discrimination is largely the result of personal prejudice and is, in general, deliberate. Individual discrimination takes place when an individual, acting on his or her own part, chooses to discriminate against another person. Institutional discrimination, on the other hand, as Nieto (1992) has explained, "is manifested through established laws, customs, and practices that reflect and reproduce . . . inequalities in society" (p. 22). In other words, because of societal pressures, assumptions, and traditions, it is entirely possible (and, indeed, not uncommon) for an individual who is not personally prejudiced to engage in institutionally discriminatory behavior. This is why, in part, members of historically oppressed groups can themselves sometimes contribute to further discrimination once they become part of "the system," and it is institutional discrimination that in many ways poses the greatest threat for us as educators. The concern of TQE with "expanding the mind-set" is thus crucial here, because it is essential that we learn to view things from perspectives that may be quite different from those that we have always taken for granted.

Further, it is important, especially in the American context, for us to keep in mind that institutional discrimination can take place either formally or informally. Formal institutional discrimination takes place where we are dealing with officially sanctioned policy, such as Jim Crow laws in the American South or apartheid in South Africa. For the most part, such formal institutional discrimination has been eliminated in the United States, and where it continues to exist, legal remedies are available. Informal institutional discrimination is, however, another matter. Informal institutional discrimination, which includes generally unarticulated values, beliefs, attitudes, procedures, and structures that permeate social and educational institutions, is far more difficult to identify and to eliminate than is formal institutional discrimination. As the Task Force on the Administration of Military Justice in the Armed Forces noted,

> Institutional discrimination refers to the effects of inequalities that are rooted in the system-wide operation of a society and have little relation to racially related attitudinal factors or the majority group's racial or ethnic prejudices. It involves "policies or practices which appear to be neutral in their effect on minority individuals or groups but which have the effect of disproportionately impacting upon them in harmful or negative ways." (Quoted in Gollnick & Chinn, 1990, pp. 90-91)

Examples of institutional discrimination abound, both in society at large and in our educational institutions. In the context of the public schools, examples of institutional discrimination include the following:

- Classroom games and activities that involve gender-based teams ("the boys against the girls," and so on)
- Disproportionate attention (either positive or negative) to members of certain groups (for example, different questioning strategies and behaviors for boys and girls, more criticism of African American than white students, and so on)
- Disproportionate and inappropriate differences in student placement related to student gender, ethnicity, race, and so on
- Toleration of comments or behaviors by some students that are offensive to others (sometimes called the "boys will be boys" problem)
- Inclusion of inappropriate, offensive, or otherwise problematic material related to gender, race, ethnicity, religion, and so on, in the curriculum (such as the presence of Christmas trees in the classroom) or the exclusion of relevant and appropriate material related to gender, race, ethnicity, religion, and so on

The list, of course, could be far longer than this; what is provided here are merely examples for reflection. For example, Nieto has identified nine structures in education in which prejudice and discrimination play important roles and which may affect student learning in significant (and negative) ways (see Figure 2.4). Nieto (1992) compellingly argues that

> the discrimination that children face in schools is not a thing of the past. School practices and policies still continue to discriminate against some children in very concrete ways. . . . For example, schools that serve students of color tend to provide curricula that are watered down and at a lower level than those that serve primarily White students. In addition, the faculty of these schools tends to have less experience and less education than colleagues who teach in schools that serve primarily European Americans and middle class students. (p. 24)

- Tracking
- Testing
- Curriculum
- Pedagogy
- Physical structure
- Disciplinary policies
- Limited role of students
- Limited role of teachers
- Limited role of parents

Figure 2.4. Educational Structures in Which Prejudice and Discrimination Affect Student Learning

We turn now to a discussion of some of the principal targets of discrimination in our society and educational institutions.

Racism, Sexism, Ageism, and Beyond

Prejudice and discrimination occur with respect to differences of race, ethnicity, gender, language, age, physical ability/disability, and a variety of other social categories (see Figure 2.5). Prejudice and discrimination related to race are termed *racism*, prejudice and discrimination related to gender are termed *sexism*, and so on. As suggested earlier in this chapter, any time that individuals or institutions categorize people or use generalizations about people as a result of a category such as gender, race, ethnicity, and so on, in a manner that is, or for reasons that are, inappropriate, then those persons have been the victims of prejudice and discrimination.

Many writers on issues related to racism in particular have argued that racism entails more than simply prejudice or discrimination. Rather, racism entails prejudice and/or discrimination supported by differential power relationships in society. Thus it would make little sense to talk about African-American racism targeting white Americans, because in our society the power base is, for the most part, in the hands of whites (and more often than

- Age
- Ethnicity
- Gender
- Language
- Physical disability
- Race
- Religion
- Sexual orientation

Figure 2.5. Common Foci for Prejudice and Discrimination

not, white males). The same argument could, of course, be made with respect to the other "isms": women, for instance, cannot be said to be "sexist" in the same way that men can, although certainly some women may hold prejudicial attitudes about, and may behave in a discriminatory manner toward, men. To some extent, debates about whether African Americans can be racist, or whether women can be sexist, and so on, are simply semantic arguments. Underlying such arguments, however, are important issues related to the nature of racism, sexism, and so on, in our society. We turn now to a discussion of the issue of power as it relates to these matters.

Examining Discrimination and Power

Power and power relations play a key role in both the development and maintenance of different kinds of discrimination in society. As Gollnick and Chinn (1990) have suggested,

The most crucial factor in understanding racism is that the majority group has power over the minority group. This power has been used to prevent people of color from securing the prestige, power, and privilege held by whites. Racism is also practiced by some whites and their institutions to maintain a dominant-subordinate relationship with nonwhite groups. Professional educators must prevent such practices from occurring in their classrooms or schools. (p. 93)

Nieto has also stressed issues of power as they relate to discrimination in general, and institutionalized discrimination in particular. As Nieto (1992) notes,

> We need to understand the important role that *power* plays in institutional racism. It is primarily through the power of the people who control these institutions that racist policies and practices are reinforced and legitimized. Furthermore, when we understand racism as a systemic problem and not only as an individual dislike for a particular group of people, we can better understand the negative and destructive effects it can have. (p. 22)

In educational settings, an awareness of the concepts of institutionalized racism, sexism, ageism, and so on, is essential if the negative effects of such "isms" are to be countered. The elimination of personal prejudice and individual discriminatory behavior, although certainly a worthwhile goal, will not, on its own, automatically result in the elimination of institutional bias and discrimination. Indeed, to a certain extent, a focus on personal and individual issues can mask the underlying (and arguably more serious) threats posed by institutional bias.

One of the ways in which institutional bias is often manifested in the school context is under the guise of educational equality. The idea of providing all students with the same, high-quality educational experience is one that has a great deal of initial, superficial merit. The problem is that such a goal fails to take into account what are often, in our society, radically different social and economic backgrounds among different students. To be sure, high standards should be a part of every student's educational experience, and every student is entitled to the highest quality education that we can provide. Having said this, though, the way in which this notable goal can be achieved will inevitably require different means for different students. This does not necessarily mean that students must or should be "tracked"; rather, it means that educational experiences need to be individualized in a meaningful way that allows the school to take full advantage of each student's background and facilitates each student's journey on the road to becoming a truly educated person.

And how can educators begin to eliminate bias and discrimination in the context of the school? This difficult and essential matter is discussed below.

Eliminating Discrimination: Selected Activities and Approaches

Among the more effective approaches to addressing problems of bias, prejudice, and discrimination from an administrative perspective are those associated with what has been called the "human relations approach" to multicultural education (see Sleeter & Grant, 1988, pp. 89-97). The activities that are associated with the human relations approach to multicultural education share a number of common assumptions, and they are generally based on five general principles, all of which, incidentally, are totally compatible with the goals and objectives of TQE. These five principles include the following:

- Efforts to address bias, prejudice, and discrimination should be comprehensive in nature and should be consistent and school- or district-wide. This is important to ensure that the targeted individuals for the program do not receive "mixed messages."
- There is no single, correct strategy for addressing such problems, and so a wide variety of different strategies, activities, and so on should be used.
- Whenever possible, activities should be active, rather than passive, in nature. Although there is real value in disseminating information about bias, prejudice, and discrimination, merely hearing about such matters often does not result in behavioral change.

- Programs and activities should be based, whenever possible, on real-life situations and experiences, much as the philosopher John Dewey advocated with respect to learning in general.
- Every individual involved in multicultural training should have positive, successful experiences related to such training. (Sleeter & Grant, 1988, pp. 89-90)

Specific examples of how the human relations approach to multiculturalism can be used in the school context include the following:

- Provide teachers, parents, and students with accurate information and data related to specific ethnic, cultural, and linguistic groups, as well as information about the common characteristics of different groups. One important way in which this can be accomplished is to involve members of different groups in the discussions. Although exposure to factual information does not automatically lead to changes in attitudes or behaviors, it can and does provide a foundation on which such changes can take place—especially if the provision of information has involved contact with members of the groups under discussion (see Sleeter & Grant, 1988, pp. 90-91).
- The use of heterogeneous groups in cooperative and collaborative learning activities can, if properly conducted, help to lead to a reduction in stereotypes, prejudice, and discrimination. As Allport has noted, "Prejudice (unless deeply rooted in the character structure of the individual) may be reduced by *equal status* contact between majority and minority groups in the pursuit of *common goals*. The effect is greatly enhanced if this contact is sanctioned by institutional supports . . . and provided it is of the sort that leads to the perception of common interests and common humanity between members of the two groups" (Allport, 1979, p. 281, quoted in Sleeter & Grant, 1988, p. 92).

- Role-playing of various sorts can be used to help members of the socially dominant group better understand the perspectives of members of other groups, and vice versa. Such role-playing can be facilitated through the use of novels, short stories, hypothetical cases, movies, and so on (see Sleeter & Grant, 1988, pp. 93-94).

- Another way in which members of different cultural groups can learn about and interact with one another is in various kinds of community action projects (see Sleeter & Grant, 1988, pp. 94-95). Such projects can be loosely or closely related to the school, although a strong case can be made for noneducational projecds being the best for school personnel to work on, because their power and status might well interfere with the effectiveness of educationally related community action projects.

All of the types of activities discussed here are useful and valuable, but it is very important to note that they are all essentially focused on the individual, rather than on social and institutional factors. Although helping individuals to become less prejudiced, and although reducing the likelihood of any particular individual behaving in a discriminatory manner are important, they are best understood not as means in and of themselves but rather as means to a far more significant end. Social justice and the elimination of institutional bias in our society, not to mention several of the central theses involved in TQE, require not just changes in individual attitudes and behaviors, but they also require that we address the issues of power, structures, and so on, in our institutions.

Key Terms and Concepts

Ageism. Ageism refers to prejudicial attitudes and/or discriminatory behavior related to an individual's age.

Discrimination. Discrimination basically refers to the process of differentiating individuals or groups and thus is not intrinsically a bad thing. However, in general usage when we talk about "discrimination," we are referring to inappropriate differentiations among groups or individuals. Discrimination involves actions or behaviors, taken either by an individual, a group, an organization, or an institution.

Institutional racism. Institutional racism refers to laws, customs, and practices that result in systematic discrimination against individuals and groups on account of their race. The presence of institutional racism does not necessarily entail the presence of individual prejudice.

Institutional sexism. Institutional sexism refers to laws, customs, and practices that result in systematic discrimination against individuals and groups on account of their gender. The presence of institutional sexism does not necessarily entail the presence of individual prejudice.

Prejudice. Prejudice refers to a negative view of or attitude about an entire group of people, usually based on stereotypes. In essence, prejudice involves the prejudging of individuals based on their membership in a specific cultural, racial, ethnic, religious, linguistic, or whatever, community.

Racism. Racism refers to prejudicial attitudes and/or discriminatory behavior related to an individual's race. Some people argue that an important component of racism is that of relative power relations; thus, although some African-Americans may have prejudicial attitudes about members of other groups, and may even engage in discriminatory behavior toward those groups, because of the relative power relations in our society, they could not be said to the "racist."

Sexism. Sexism refers to prejudicial attitudes and/or discriminatory behavior related to an individual's gender.

Sociotype. Sociotypes are accurate generalizations about social, racial, ethnic, linguistic, and cultural groups and can be distinguished from stereotypes, which are inaccurate generalizations.

Stereotype. Stereotypes are inaccurate or dangerous generalizations about social, ethnic, racial, linguistic, and cultural groups. Such generalizations can be either positive (e.g., "All Asians are good at math") or negative (e.g., "All Irish-Americans are prone to drinking heavily") in nature.

References

Allport, G. (1979). *The nature of prejudice*. Reading, MA: Addison-Wesley.

Bennett, C. (1990). *Comprehensive multicultural education: Theory and practice* (2nd ed.). Boston: Allyn & Bacon.

Garcia, R. (1982). *Teaching in a pluralistic society: Concepts, models, strategies*. New York: Harper & Row.

Gollnick, D., & Chinn, P. (1990). *Multicultural education in a pluralistic society* (3rd ed.). New York: Merrill.

Nieto, S. (1992). *Affirming diversity: The sociopolitical context of multicultural education*. New York: Longman.

Sleeter, C., & Grant, C. (1988). *Making choices for multicultural education: Five approaches to race, class, and gender*. Columbus, OH: Merrill.

✧ 3 ✧

Eliminating Structural Barriers That Limit Student Access

In the previous chapter we discussed Sonia Nieto's argument that some school practices and policies negatively affect student learning. In this chapter we identify some of these practices and relate them to second-generation discrimination.

Second-Generation Discrimination

Kenneth Meier and Joseph Stewart (1991) studied the struggle of African Americans and Hispanics in achieving equal access to education. They use the term *second-generation discrimination* to describe the "series of actions that school districts can take to limit minority student access to education" (p. 1). Meier and Stewart include discipline and academic grouping in second-generation discrimination. In this chapter we expand discrimination to include teaching practices; curriculum; testing issues; lack of empowerment of students, teachers, and families; and the school facility itself. Instructing educators in the subtleties of second-generation discrimination is far more complex than making them aware of first-generation discrimination with its blatant segregation of students.

Eliminating Fundamental Barriers to Access

When exploring the many barriers of student access to education, we must keep in mind the conflicting goals found in schools. The school administrator plays a key role in creating the vision of what the school is trying to achieve and must be sure to remind colleagues of these potentially conflicting goals. These may include the following:

- Academic grouping practices in direct contrast to the goals of integration
- Seeking unity among groups of people versus the need to affirm uniqueness of each group
- Testing to diagnose and place students versus relegating students to immutable tracks
- Disciplinary policies that are crucial to the safety and orderliness of schools but are enforced in a manner that encourages discrimination and unequal access

Researchers have found strong relationships between the political influence of groups and the access of those groups to educational equity. Thus, although we focus here on what schools can do to increase access for students from different racial and ethnic groups, schools play a secondary role to the power inherent in political groups such as school boards, and local and state government. It is the administrator's job to educate these groups, particularly because they are often not proportionately representative of the racial/ethnic groups of their constituents.

Academic Groupings

Grouping can be homogeneous (one ability level) or heterogeneous (mixed ability levels). In recent years, schools have begun to examine their grouping practices because of the overwhelming

evidence that homogeneous grouping can have a long-term negative impact on some children and that there is little, if any, justification for this grouping. Ability grouping, often referred to as
tracking, occurs at any grade level including preschool. Ability
grouping is manifested in schools in ways such as

- Special education classes
- Gifted/talented programs
- Honors classes
- Vocation, general, business, and college tracks
- Reading, mathematics, and other ability groups
- Bilingual programs

Ability grouping practices will not always negatively affect students, but in view of the inherent dangers, TQE administrators
should ask the following questions of such practices:

- What evidence exists that these students should be placed
  in special education classes?
- What evidence exists that the school needs to offer two,
  three, or four levels of English?
- What evidence exists that elementary homogeneous reading groups will benefit children?
- What alternatives to our current tracking practices exist?

Studying data from classrooms around the country, Meier and
Stewart (1991) found that (a) Hispanics are 20% more likely to be
assigned to educable mentally retarded (EMR) classes than are
students in general and (b) Hispanics and African Americans have
limited access to gifted classes. Their research also suggests that
(a) grouping is used to handle disciplinary problems, (b) bilingual
education limits Hispanic access to equal education opportunities, and (c) ethnic disparities in gifted class enrollment are
increasing.

Discipline

Most research studies regarding discipline focus on corporal punishment, suspensions, and expulsions. Empirical data on the number of referrals to the principal's office for discipline issues or the verbal reprimand of students have only been studied in limited ways. Thus the long-term impact of such practices on students of various racial/ethnic groups is unknown. There is considerable evidence to support the conclusion that discipline is often used for purposes other than to maintain order in a school building. In their synthesis of the research Meier and Stewart report the following:

- Hispanic students are more likely to receive corporal punishment than Anglo students.
- Puerto Ricans are 43% overrepresented among students expelled from school.
- As the African American suspension rate increases, the relative level of suspension among Hispanics decreases.
- African American students are suspended for offenses that are often permitted to Anglo students.
- Dress codes are more rigidly enforced against Hispanic students than Anglo students.

Recommendations for the TQE Administrator are the following:

- Keep a record of who is referred to the office, disaggregating the data by racial/ethnic group.
- Examine data on suspensions and expulsions to see if some groups are overrepresented.
- Examine the reasons for teacher referrals to see if there are differences for various racial/ethnic groups.

Selectively punishing students from various racial/ethnic groups can discourage them from attending school or encourage them to rebel against school policies, procedures, and adults in authority.

Another area not fully examined in the literature is the long-term impact of classroom management. Many classroom management models are authoritarian in nature and are therefore in conflict with the theory of placing responsibility for individual actions on the child. As we discuss in chapter 4, it is the subtle and not-so-subtle messages given to children by the school that are part of the unintended or hidden curriculum. These messages may affect students as much, if not more than, the intended curriculum goals.

The School Building: Inviting or Prisonlike

It is not just a humorous comment made by children that school often makes them feel as if they are in jail. The reality is that the environment of far too many schools is indeed more similar to a penal institution than a place that enhances student learning. For many children, school is a refuge and should be a safe haven from outside dangers. To ensure that the school building is inviting, the environment itself must be intellectually stimulating. School administrators who are conscious of the importance of the environment will ask the following:

- Is the school's landscape design and the community part of the total learning environment?
- Does the school provide a safe and clean setting?
- Does the school have signs providing directions for guests?
- Are alternatives to the use of dogs by school guards or the police to sniff out drugs considered?
- Are school doors unlocked so that visitors can easily enter?
- Are police frequently in the school?
- Are there school guards and administrators visible in the corridors using their walkie-talkies?
- Are students, teachers, families, and guests able to find parking?
- Are school lots unlocked so that people are able to leave without someone unlocking the fence?
- Do classrooms have windows?

- Is graffiti removed on a regular basis?
- Do students throw trash all over the building?
- Are desks nailed to the floor?
- Does the school's architecture provide areas for growing plants, using water for science, art, and so on?
- Is the playground free of debris such as shards of glass, litter, and drug paraphernalia?
- Is the building properly lit inside? Outside?
- Does the school have good ventilation or is it airless?
- Do heating and air-conditioning systems work properly?
- Are toilets broken? Is there toilet paper?
- Does the school have a child-care center where students can learn parenting skills?
- If there is playground equipment, is it well maintained?
- Does the school have adequate technology?
- Was the school constructed properly for the grade levels it serves, or is there a mismatch between the physical layout of buildings and the children who inhabit them?
- Is there an easy access to toilets for students with handicaps?
- Are classrooms and corridors painted appealing colors rather than drab institutional colors?

The answers to the questions above reveal much about the culture of the school and how inviting it is for all students.

If schools are adding or constructing new facilities, the teams involved in the planning must consider cultural diversity. Schools and classrooms should use space in symbolic ways congruent with the value systems appreciated by the cultures of the community. For example, some cultures place much value on nature. They may want parts of buildings to be separated to take advantage of the local setting. In other communities, certain styles of architecture, such as Cape Cod cedar shingles or earthen-colored adobe may help reinforce a sense of heritage or community. Thus, when designing learning environments, knowing how the school's cultural groups symbolically perceive the setting and the things in it is critical to making appropriate inclusions or eliminations.

Testing Issues

Testing is another barrier that may impede educational equity. Since *A Nation at Risk* was published in 1983, an increasing number of states have introduced statewide testing programs in addition to the already staggering number of standardized tests taken by schoolchildren. Test results tend to classify or sort students into categories that may impede educational equity. Questions the TQE Administrator needs to ask include the following:

- Are the tests bias-free?
- Are achievement tests used to sort students?
- What long-term impact do the results of these tests have on students from various racial/ethnic backgrounds?
- Because of test results, are teachers forced to teach to the test?
- Do test outcomes result in more remediation rather than acceleration?
- How, if at all, do students benefit from the testing?
- Are test results the main or only criteria for student placement in classes, groups, or tracks?

The Curriculum

Another area where discriminatory practices can be found is in the curriculum itself. There is often a mismatch between what is taught and the appropriateness of what students need to learn. For example, the "just say no" focus of many assembly talks or class visitors does not help students to deal with the day-to-day challenges they face. Instead, our focus should more closely align with the reality of students' lives. How do youths deal with this issue when they are getting pressured by a peer? What skills do they need? How can the school provide a nonthreatening forum for controversial issues to be discussed?

In addition to the possible mismatch or inappropriateness of some curriculum, four crucial curricular aspects may reinforce limited perspectives, discriminatory behaviors, and stereotypes. They include the following:

1. Textbooks and other materials
2. The school year and schedule
3. Curriculum policies and practices
4. The artificial division of the curriculum into subject areas

Chapter 2 explored the discrimination found in some teaching materials. Although today students will more likely find images of themselves reflected in photographs and pictures, Anglos continue to dominate textbooks. In addition, textbooks rarely discuss the complexity of controversial issues such as race, gender, and discrimination. Educators need to closely monitor written materials to safeguard against what are often superficial perspectives on issues of cultural diversity.

Although educators often do not consider how schools structure time as a component of the curriculum, the use of time is a crucial variable in student learning. As Goodlad (1984) states in his classic *A Place Called School*, "The availability of time . . . sets the basic framework for learning. After that, how this time is used becomes a significant factor in students' accomplishment" (p. 97). The U.S. public school calendar is an anachronism. Because we are no longer an agrarian nation (and have not been for a over 100 years), a school calendar that provides little opportunity for children to study for 3 months in the summer is clearly nonresponsive to the needs of children and society. A school infused with the tenets of TQE will question the value of how the school year, week, and day are structured by asking questions such as, Does a longer summer break result in student loss of knowledge? What impact does the summer break have on students with disabilities or on language minority students?

Another aspect of the use of time that needs to be challenged is the school schedule. Most high schools have five, six, or seven class periods. Classes are approximately 40 to 45 minutes in length, and most core classes are offered for one period a day, 5 days a week. Is there research that supports these school schedules? Are there more appropriate formats for scheduling classes? Is this the best format for teaching this content?

TQE administrators need to ask the following:

- What does research say about the optimal learning time for children at this age level?
- Do we need to offer this class on a daily basis?
- Is it necessary for children to have a different teacher each year or can the teacher move with the children?
- Some private schools in the United States and public schools in other nations schedule school 6 days a week; why do we have a 5-day school week and a 180-day school calendar?

Another aspect that may result in limiting student access is curriculum policies and practices. For example, some schools may limit student access by not allowing a 7th or 8th grader to study a language other than English if the student has not attained a certain reading level in English. What evidence exists that students who have not attained that reading level would be hurt by studying another language? In reality, no evidence has yet been found. Instead, the opportunity to study a second language improves many English language skills as well as the motivation of the learner.

Usually free and reduced-price lunches and breakfast programs are not thought of as part of the curriculum. However, all the planned activities of a school are part of the curriculum. Even a school district's policy of offering free and reduced-price lunches or breakfast could have a negative impact on children from culturally diverse backgrounds. For example, a relatively small urban school district in New England decided not to offer a free-breakfast program to its students, challenging a state law that requires a school district to offer a breakfast program if at least 80% of the students qualify for federally funded subsidized lunches. Several of the school board members felt the law to be unfair and believed that parents, not the schools, should be responsible for feeding their children. The reality is that children were going to school hungry, no matter what the school board members believe parents should do. Systemic thinking is a requirement if an organization is striving to be a learning organization. Denying children breakfast because one believes that "good" parents should provide breakfast is an example of issue avoidance.

TQE should expand the mind-set. If multicultural education is to be successful, it requires new perspectives and insights into all parts of the educational process, including policies on lunch and breakfast.

The artificial division of the curriculum into content areas is another fundamental issue that can serve as a barrier to student access to knowledge. Nearly every high school in the country offers mathematics, science, history, languages, and English, which divides knowledge into discrete areas. Algebra 1 tends to be taught in 9th grade, 10th-grade students usually take geometry, and 11th graders are offered Algebra 2. Why is the mathematics program structured this way? Why does physics usually follow chemistry? If we were to examine the curricular offerings of many other nations, we would find that strands of each science or math area are woven throughout courses at various grade levels. Thus a 9th grader in another country may have some biology, chemistry, or physics all in 1 year. Unless schools integrate curriculum to connect various disciplines, it will continue to be difficult for students to make "intuitive leaps" in their knowledge gaps.

Teaching Practices

In recent years cognitive scientists describe the learning process as "constructivist." With a constructivist approach to learning, students play active roles in constructing or developing their own learning. This is in contrast to tradition where students have been considered empty vessels who passively absorb knowledge presented by teachers. Students were required to memorize facts, take tests, and follow a drill and practice routine. Teachers taught the essential information that all students needed to know; competition was the expected mode of learning.

Inherent in constructivism is the idea of sense making. The student seeks to make sense of the curriculum presented, whereas the teacher's role is to facilitate the sense making. Because constructivists believe that sense making is influenced by the perceptions of the understanding of others, it is crucial for schools to ensure that a variety of perspectives are presented to students.

Also, inherent in constructivism is the notion that the meaning of the curriculum is socially negotiated. The textbook is no longer presented as a fixed body of information with a singular meaning. Instead, knowledge becomes subjective and evolving. For example, in studying the American Civil War, the teacher's role should be to help students critically analyze views present in the textbook. The teacher might add views not presented by reading letters written from soldiers to their parents or from a relative in the South to one in the North. As students connect pieces of knowledge, a more authentic understanding is attained. This is directly related to the issue discussed earlier of the lack of curriculum integration in most schools. Seeing relations across disciplines is difficult for students, thus their construction of reality is limited.

How teachers believe learning is constructed and how diversity can effect learning should be the centerpiece of dialogue in the preparation of teachers as well as in professional development. A constructivist approach to teaching is congruent with the concepts of TQE because both share the notion of continuous learning. A school that is striving for continuous improvement will, on an ongoing basis, focus on improvement in terms of people's sensitivity to, and recognition of, the diversity within the school, the community, and in society.

The Limited Roles of Teachers, Students, and Families

Inherent in a constructivist view of education is the empowerment of students, teachers, and families. The hierarchical decision making traditionally found in American schools has perpetuated and supported the notion that administrators tell teachers what they should do. Teachers must do what they are told to do, and students and families should do what teachers tell them to do. However, in a truly democratic school community, teachers, students, and families will be invited to actively participate by questioning, sharing, reflecting, and challenging.

According to TQE, schools should focus on students' innate "yearning for learning" (Bostingl, 1993). This requires that schools find instruments of commonality, collaboration, and democratic ways of understanding, which can be translated into the continuous improvement of student learning.

In multicultural education, perhaps the best examples of mechanisms for enhancing the child's primary learning experiences can be found in the research of Luis Moll (1988) and Jim Cummins (1986). These researchers maintain that students from diverse cultural backgrounds are not often engaged on multiple levels. Thus they are denied the opportunity to weave experiences and knowledge of their language, culture, and communities into their classroom learning. Moll (1988) asked the question, How can we use the diverse resources found in multicultural schools to promote equity and facilitate quality? He found that the most effective classes for Latino students were those taught by teachers who encouraged students to use personal experiences to make sense of their school experience.

Moll's research underscores that in most classrooms, home and community experiences are avoided. However, when home knowledge is valued, positive effects are realized. Moll (1988) maintains that "all communities contain a wealth of knowledge and skills which can be recognized and used by schools to facilitate instruction" (p. 468). This premise, suggesting that there are "funds of knowledge" available in the community that can be made relevant to classroom instruction, is the basis of Moll's community knowledge classroom practice project. The goal of this project was to use these funds of knowledge to create classroom settings where students are immersed in literacy activities that are culturally appropriate and intellectually challenging. For example, in one community many parents were carpenters and home builders. These family members were invited to the school to relate principles of mathematics to building homes, thus increasing the cultural relevance of instruction.

A basic understanding of the concept of second-generation discrimination is critical to the TQE administrator in ensuring that such obstacles to learning by students of various racial and cultural groups are avoided.

Key Terms and Concepts

EMR. This acronym stands for educable mentally retarded; a category used to classify special education students.

Second-generation discrimination. According to Meier and Stewart it is the use of academic grouping and discipline in a discriminatory manner.

References

Bostingl, J. J. (1993). Creating total quality schools. *Association for Supervision and Curriculum Development, 35*(2), 4-7.

Cummins, J. (1986). Empowering minority students: A framework for intervention. *Harvard Educational Review, 56*(1), 18-36.

Goodlad, J. I. (1984). *A place called school.* New York: McGraw-Hill.

Meier, K. J., & Stewart, J. (1991). *The politics of Hispanic education: Un paso pálante y dos pátras.* Albany, NY: State University of New York Press.

Moll, L. C. (1988). Some key issues in teaching Latino students. *Language Arts, 65*(5), 465-472.

The National Commission on Excellence in Education (1983). *A nation at risk: The imperative for educational reform.* Washington, D.C.: U.S. Department of Education.

✦ 4 ✦

Enhancing Staff and
Curriculum Development

This chapter describes how cultural diversity affects staff and curriculum development. First, we summarize factors that comprise diversity and focus on the school administrator as a role model for the school community. This is followed by a discussion of how administrators can assist teachers in becoming culturally responsive in their teaching and the roles of other staff members— paraprofessionals, nonteaching faculty, secretaries, custodians, cafeteria workers, and bus drivers among others—in promoting diversity. Following a discussion of curriculum issues in relation to equity and cultural diversity, we conclude the chapter with suggestions of how *all* staff members can increase their knowledge about issues of cultural diversity.

Diversity in Schools

All schools have some diversity in their staff and student populations, whether they are located in upstate New York or along the Rio Grande Valley, or whether a school is predominately of one racial/ethnic group or consists of a variety of cultural groups. Differences may include age, gender, socioeconomic status, mental ability, physical ability, sexual orientation, religion, language, and ethnicity. It is a myth for an educator to say that his or

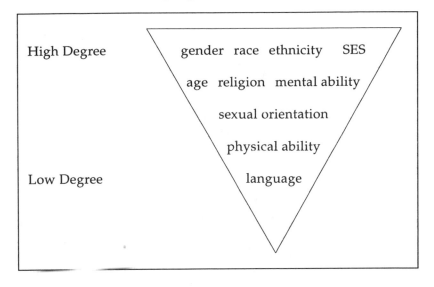

Figure 4.1. Factors Comprising Cultural Diversity

her school is not, in some ways, diverse. Although some schools have greater diversity than others, *all* schools must acknowledge and act on the diversity found in their populations, the community itself, the state, the nation, and our planet. Therefore, staff and students need to (a) be aware of diversity, (b) have knowledge and understanding about that diversity, and (c) take action based on that awareness and knowledge—*praxis.*

Depending on the student, some factors may play a far more important role than others. In Figure 4.1 we list the various diversity factors that can be found in a school's population. The greater the number of factors, the greater the amount of diversity in the school. For example, an inner-city school with a student population of all African American students, who are from a low socioeconomic background, may have *less* diversity than a typical suburban school. Many educators, when talking about culturally diverse schools, assume that urban schools are the most heterogeneous. The words *diversity, urban,* and *minority student* are *not* synonymous.

Administrators: Role Models of Praxis

The notion of a school administrator as the head teacher is an important metaphor to remember. Peter Senge (1991) discusses the importance of organizations focusing on learning in which leaders are responsible for helping people to continually expand "their capabilities to shape their future" (p. 12). If administrators are to lead learning organizations, they need to be what Senge calls "designers, teachers, and stewards." As head teacher, the school administrator is a role model for staff members, students, families, and the community. School administrators must communicate ideas with clarity and model the implementation of these ideas.

Praxis, a term used by one of our century's great educational thinkers, Paulo Freire (1970), refers to the process of connecting reflection with action while pursuing knowledge and social change. It is through praxis that a school administrator can provide equity of opportunity for all students in the school. To provide equity for all students, TQE administrators should ask themselves the following questions: Have I

- Encouraged the recruitment and selection of staff representing various racial, ethnic, and other cultural groups?
- Worked to become well-informed on the broad concepts of cultural diversity and equity?
- Encouraged staff to become aware of and sensitive to cultural issues?
- Provided training for staff in issues of cultural diversity?
- Reviewed brochures, fliers, the mission statement, and other relevant documents to ensure equity for all members of the school community?
- Encouraged colleagues to attend conferences or workshops on issues of cultural diversity and equity?
- Provided orientation for the board or other groups in the school and encouraged them to adopt a supportive policy statement?
- Given recognition to those colleagues who have taken affirmative action to implement concepts of cultural diversity and equity in the school?

- Consciously avoided any implications that cultural diversity and equity are concepts being implemented for minority groups, women, and people with disabilities rather than a basic component of a quality educational program for all?
- Worked toward resolving conflicts among staff members who may disagree on the concepts and procedures related to cultural diversity and equity?
- Encouraged the staff to have the school reflect cultural diversity with photographs, videos, brochures, and other visible items?
- Communicated strong support for cultural diversity regardless of the makeup of the ethnic/racial/cultural groups served by the school?
- Raised issues of cultural diversity and equity at staff meetings?
- Provided assistance to staff members who are having difficulty accepting or implementing multicultural concepts?
- Examined school policies, programs, and documents to see whether stereotypes are being reinforced?
- Reviewed memos/presentations/letters to ensure against relaying sexist or culturally biased messages?
- Presented a positive role model for colleagues in dealing with diverse populations?
- Communicated or interacted differently with colleagues of different sexes? Ethnic groups? Disabilities? Religions?
- Communicated with the library media staff about the acquisition of multicultural education resource materials for students, staff, and families?
- Communicated with community groups regarding the objectives of a multicultural education program?
- Provided opportunities for staff to share successes and challenges in implementing a multicultural curriculum?
- Ensured that the school is a caring community that recognizes and celebrates who students and staff members are?
- Included multicultural goals as part of the staff's regular planning and performance appraisals?

Culturally Responsive Teaching

As is clear from the foregoing, school administrators must, in addition to modeling, provide leadership by facilitating the efforts of staff members. An effective teacher must be prepared to work with children from various racial/ethnic groups. Most preparation programs afford teacher education students the opportunity to study the foundations of what makes a teacher effective; however, their classes are typically based on research that is traditionally ethnocentric in focus. There are very few homogeneous classrooms in existence today, and all teachers need to be prepared to use a variety of instructional practices and strategies. Although teacher education programs are beginning to recognize the importance of preparing students to teach in culturally diverse classrooms, many recent graduates have minimal knowledge and skill in these issues of diversity. As a consequence, school administrators must assist not only veteran teachers in recognizing the importance of culturally responsive teaching but must also remember that many recent graduates are lacking skills in this area as well.

The relatively poor academic achievement of some racial/ethnic groups (e.g., Native Americans, Puerto Ricans, African Americans) is already well documented. What seems less understood is why their school failure persists and what teachers can do about it. It is critical for school personnel to understand the research on the academic success of various cultural groups because ethnic minorities currently constitute over 20% of the school-age population. Projections for the year 2000 estimate that over 40% of the school-age population will come from various racial/ethnic groups. According to Christine Sleeter (1992), at the same time trends show "that by the year 2000 only about 5% of the nation's teaching force will be people of color" (p. 208). Similar statistics apply to school administrators.

The challenge for administrators is to assist classroom teachers in improving their understanding of cultures, both their own and those of their students. Because one of the themes of total quality education is continuous improvement, it is crucial that school administrators assist teachers in increasing their knowledge of diversity issues. TQE administrators can facilitate teachers' understanding of issues of cultural diversity in the following ways:

- Encourage teachers to explore the cultures to which they belong.
- Allocate professional development monies for teachers to gain specific knowledge about the broad cultural patterns and individual and local variations of the children in their classes.
- Provide opportunities for teachers to collaborate with other educators representing various racial/ethnic groups or teachers working with highly diverse populations.
- Allocate resources for training in areas of cultural diversity, human relations, working with parents, and related areas.
- Ensure that during teacher training workshops and times set aside for less formal staff development, teachers interact with each other and discuss how they might handle particular issues.
- Hold discussions regarding books that describe racial/ethnic experiences (e.g., Nicholas Lemann's *The Promised Land*, Alex Kotlowitz's There Are No Children Here) or books written by members of racial/ethnic groups (e.g., Toni Morrison's works, Luis Rodriguez's *Always Running*, Cornel West's *Race Matters*).
- Assist teachers in determining what kinds of interaction they permit or encourage in their classrooms (e.g., encourage peer observation systems, audio cassettes, or videotape recordings).
- Ensure that teachers have positive attitudes toward themselves, their students, and the potential their students can attain.
- Assist teachers in communicating with parents as well as in establishing program goals.
- Facilitate opportunities for teachers to become involved with religious, civic, and community organizations as well as businesses.
- Provide release time for teachers to meet with parents when it is convenient for both.
- Ensure that teachers interact with all students in their classes, providing equal opportunity for all students to receive teacher time and attention.

- Encourage the use of a variety of teaching styles that allow for a variety of learning styles.

Enhancing Diversity: The Roles of Classified Staff Members

As discussed in chapter 1, TQE emphasizes teamwork and the empowerment of all people in the school. Too often school administrators forget the vast potential of classified staff members in creating an inviting culture in a school. Secretaries, library personnel, guidance personnel, social workers, school psychologists, assessment specialists, bus drivers, teacher aides, cafeteria workers, custodians, school nurses, and school volunteers often interact with more children on a daily basis than do some teachers. Many of the suggestions for facilitating cultural understanding for teachers also apply to nonteaching personnel; however, other strategies are unique to these groups. Suggestions for assisting nonteaching personnel in working with culturally diverse children and adults include the following:

- Direct appropriate nonteaching staff to assist teachers in asking community members to act as informants about language use in the home, verbal interaction, and so on.
- Assist teachers in setting up a personal information profile of their classroom teaching (e.g., helping teachers to record their patterns of interaction).
- Visit homes and conduct observations (of cultural language patterns, etc.) outside school.
- Provide professional development for training in areas that are related to cultural diversity.
- Ensure that nonteaching staff are included in all appropriate school activities including committees and decision-making teams.
- Hire nonteaching staff who have had experience in working in culturally diverse environments.
- Hire nonteaching staff who represent the ethnic/racial groups found in the school or the community's population.

- Ensure that the social worker, the school psychologist, and/or guidance personnel play integral roles in the overall structure of the school (especially in communicating with parents and other school personnel).

Focusing on the Curriculum

Many teachers become apprehensive when they hear the words *multicultural curriculum* because they think they will need to add more information to their already overburdened curriculum. First, we must remember that curriculum is more than the courses or content areas that students are required to take. The learning that takes place outside class, in the corridors, the playground, or at the meeting of a school club, is also a part of the curriculum. There is also the hidden curriculum that includes the norms, beliefs, and values about the social relations of school and classroom life that are transmitted to students. Developing a multicultural perspective is important for students in schools that are in multicultural settings as well as in those in a more homogeneous environment.

If we define curriculum as all the experiences provided the student under the direction of the school, then it becomes evident that we are discussing a philosophy of multiculturalism rather than multicultural education as an additional course, a book in a curriculum, or a picture on a bulletin board. Administrators should have as their goal that all staff members work with children from a multicultural perspective.

Teaching From a Multicultural Perspective

Many people who write about multicultural education use the terms *stages* or *levels* to describe the progression as a school moves toward being truly multicultural in its teaching. Some schools focus on the contributions of various racial/ethnic groups by celebrating school holidays, heroines and heroes, or specific accomplishments of a particular group. Examples might include the following: celebrating Cinco de Mayo, holding an ethnic foods celebration, having children draw flags of other countries for display, adding Rosa Parks and Martin Luther King to the social studies curriculum, or including the study of Mayan pyramids. Although these activities in and of themselves may be appropriate, if they are the only parts of the curriculum that celebrate diversity, then the goal of teaching from a multicultural perspective will not be accomplished.

Another approach taken by many schools is to add courses to the curriculum without altering the philosophy of teaching or the content of the program area. Examples might include adding a course in Latin American literature, teaching students how to use an abacus, or adding information to the algebra curriculum about the contributions made by Arab mathematicians. There is nothing wrong with any of these initiatives, but the structure of the overall program has not been changed.

According to James Banks (1987), who has done considerable writing on multicultural curriculum, the structure of the curriculum must be changed to allow students to view issues from a variety of perspectives. Banks proposes that the main goal of multicultural education should be to help students develop decision-making and social action skills. By doing this, students learn to view activities and events from a variety of perspectives. If the content of the curriculum is presented from a variety of perspectives, then the student will be forced to construct his or her reality of the event or situation. Inherent in this approach to multicultural education is a restructuring of the curriculum.

A challenge for school administrators is to ensure that the school works toward empowering teachers and students to make informed decisions about what teachers will teach and how students will construct what is taught. This is tied to another theme found in TQE: expanding the mind-set. To ensure that the curriculum is progressing toward this goal, the following questions should be explored:

- Does the curriculum reflect the cultural diversity of the school and the school system?
- Are media collections appropriate to the cultural diversity of the school and the school system?

- Do assessment procedures and testing materials recognize cultural differences?
- Do school assemblies and other activities highlight and include participation of all racial/ethnic groups in the school or the school system?
- Do appropriate and well-publicized multicultural goals-exist?
- Are the goals expressed in observable ways (e.g., students see images of themselves in school brochures, newspapers, yearbooks)?
- Are school facilities clean and inviting places where all students feel safe and respected?
- Do all committees, clubs, councils, and so on, of students, parents, staff, and community members have proportionate ethnic, gender, and racial representation?
- Are instructional materials free of bias?
- Do instructional materials promote respect for cultural differences?
- Is time arranged for teachers and staff to work on curriculum development efforts that would enhance the multicultural education thrust?
- Does the library have reading materials that represent the works of writers from all around the world?
- Does the school have an infrastructure that offers all students opportunities to vent, to explore, to discuss, and to create opportunities for sharing with others, and so on?
- Does the professional development committee have a diverse ethnic and racial composition? Do this committee's goals specifically address multicultural issues?
- Does the curriculum include emphasis on democracy, equity, multiple perspectives, and so on? Are students allowed to present differing viewpoints?
- Are the achievements of women scientists, engineers, and so on, and those who are of various racial/ethnic groups included in the curriculum?

- Are curricular areas integrated so that opportunities for issues of related themes and cultural diversity can be connected, thereby helping students to have a better understanding of the whole?

Increasing Knowledge About Issues of Diversity

Given that the typical classroom teacher and school administrator come from middle-class, Anglo backgrounds, learning about children from the myriad of cultures found in schools today is a continuing challenge. Continuous education and training is inherent in a school that promotes the tenets of total quality education. Rather than viewing issues of cultural diversity as something else we have to know about, we should work toward making it a part of the reflection and ongoing dialogue that should permeate a school community. Listed below are activities for TQE administrators and staff that will enhance the dialogue and reflection:

- Explore the community or part of town where students from racial/ethnic backgrounds reside.
- Select a particular ethnic/religious/racial group and learn as much as you can about that group.
- Visit ethnic restaurants, bakeries, shops, local art galleries, theaters, museums, and so on.
- Explore your family history.
- Study a language for fun, making your goal conversational fluency.
- Read local newspapers geared toward these cultural groups.
- Watch videos such as "El Norte" (it is in English), "Ethnic Notions," and so on.
- Read books about different cultures.
- Begin ongoing student and teacher exchanges with an urban/ suburban school.
- Organize an international school exchange.

- Create a students' human rights committee that brings in speakers (i.e., topics such as racism).
- Be aware of the language you use. Avoid sexist terms. Many words that were previously acceptable to describe racial/ethnic groups are no longer acceptable.
- Attend a multicultural workshop.
- Pay attention to issues of cultural diversity when you read the newspaper. Nearly every day there are articles that deal with issues of nonnative English speakers, racism, poverty, cultural traditions, gender, homosexuality, people with handicaps, and so on.
- Take a ride on an inner-city bus. Who rides the bus? What do people talk about? What is every day like for them without a car?
- Visit a church you know one of your students attends.
- Go to juvenile court and observe for a few hours.
- Put yourself in locations where you find people who belong to the particular group you are studying.
- Offer a cultural diversity day celebration including seminars, assemblies, and cultural performances.
- Offer a schoolwide multicultural "read-in."
- Invite students from a culturally diverse school to spend a day at your school. (Be sure the day has a particular focus.)
- Attend a race/culture retreat or seminar with your colleagues. Have discussions and conduct activities that get at the core of these issues. Develop a type of action plan as a follow-up to this retreat.

These suggestions are offered as a beginning for school personnel to explore the racial and ethnic groups found in their schools. Some are more appropriate for elementary personnel, whereas others focus on issues that are more important to secondary school personnel. As staff members begin to investigate issues of diversity, their enthusiasm will motivate colleagues to experiment with these and other ideas.

Key Terms and Concepts

Cultural diversity. This term refers to the presence in a particular society of different cultural groups. It is an empirical term in that it does not entail any values about the worth, or value, of diversity.

Curriculum. All the experiences provided students under the direction of the school.

Hidden curriculum. Unintentional messages that are not a part of the explicit curriculum but may affect students.

Praxis. A term used by Paulo Freire (1970) in *Pedagogy of the Oppressed* connecting reflection with action in search of knowledge and social change or justice.

References

Banks, J. A. (1987). *Teaching strategies for ethnic studies* (4th ed.). Boston: Allyn & Bacon.

Freire, P. (1970). *Pedagogy of the oppressed.* New York: Seabury.

Kotlowitz, A. (1991). *There are no children here.* New York: Doubleday.

Lemann, N. (1991). *The promised land.* New York: Alfred A. Knopf.

Rodriguez, L. (1993). *Always running: La vida loca: Gang days in L.A.* Willimantic, CT: Curbstone.

Senge, P. (1991, November). Recapturing the spirit of learning through a systems approach. *The School Administrator,* pp. 8-13.

Sleeter, C. E. (1992). *Keepers of the American dream: A study of staff development and multicultural education.* Bristol, PA: Falmer.

West, C. (1993). *Race matters.* Boston, MA: Beacon.

✧ 5 ✧

Fostering School, Community, and Family Partnerships

We begin this chapter by discussing the changing social and cultural demographics of American families, including a discussion of a new definition of *family*. We argue that in order for educators to have strong relationships with families, our notion of parent involvement must be reconceptualized. This is followed by a discussion of five categories of family involvement in schools. Next, we explore how partnerships enhance relations between schools and families. We describe the many ways to increase communication between families and schools with a special focus on culturally diverse parents. We discuss how to foster partnerships among families, schools, and communities, offering the metaphor of schools as "caring communities." Finally, we present the case for the need to find new roles for schools in working with communities and culturally diverse families.

The Changing Demographics of America's Schoolchildren

Before discussing family involvement in schools, let us take a look at the changing American family. Compared with 20 years ago, we find

- Fewer married couples with children

- More families with stepchildren
- More nonfamily households
- More teenage mothers
- More families with both parents working full-time
- More children living with single mothers
- More single fathers raising children on their own
- Many more single-parent families, especially among African Americans
- An increase in the number of children living with grandparents
- An increase in the number of gay and lesbian families
- Major gaps between the income of married-couple families by ethnicity and race and that of single-parent families
- Greater diversity in the number of children (as well as diversity of age and ethnicity) (Outtz 1993)

It is important for school personnel to recognize the diversity within single-parent families. Single parents may dramatically differ from one another with respect to

- Age when parenting began
- Income
- Personality
- Cultural heritage
- Length of time as single parent
- Support from extended family
- Reason for single parenting (e.g., divorce, death, separation, never married, etc.)
- Religious beliefs
- Sexual orientation
- Number of children

Many of these different types of families are so new that there is little, if any, research showing the effects on children. However, simply because families are different does not mean they are dysfunctional.

Given the demographic changes in our schools and the changing family, it is crucial for schools to begin addressing the unique needs of culturally diverse parents. This diversity includes language, class, race/ethnicity, children coming from nontraditional households, and so on.

Ethnic, Racial, and Cultural Factors

Included in the changing demographics of families are ethnic, racial, and cultural factors. The early part of the 17th century brought the involuntary immigration of African people to this country as slaves. By the late 1700s many southern states had large percentages of blacks added to their populations. Three great waves of voluntary immigrants followed. The first great wave of immigration reached its peak around 1820, with immigrants coming mostly from Great Britain, Ireland, Scandinavia, and Germany. At the turn of the 20th century another great wave of immigration took place with immigrants coming primarily from Southern and Eastern Europe. The newest waves of immigrants began arriving in the late 1960s, coming primarily from Asia and Latin America (see Figure 5.1). In 1985, for instance, some 80% of the total immigration was evenly divided between Mexico and Asia (Kellogg, 1988).

The population of the United States is now approximately 245 million. As of 1992, the population was 12% African American, 6.6% Hispanic, 1.6% Asian, 0.8% Native American, and the remaining 80% were Anglo. Thus there are considerable changes in the ethnicity of the children at the schoolhouse door. An additional factor is the increasing number of illegal immigrants and refugees coming to America.

Our latest newcomers have brought additional challenges. Schools now have

- Greater numbers of children whose native language is not English
- More parents coming from school systems radically different from the U.S. educational system

Newest Immigrants	Major Areas of Settlement
Latin America	California
Mexico	
El Salvador	New York
Guatemala	
Nicaragua	Texas
Honduras	
	Florida
Asia	
Vietnam	Massachusetts
Philippines	
Korea	Pennsylvania
China	
India	Michigan
Laos	
Cambodia	Ohio
Japan	

Figure 5.1. Recent Immigration to the U.S.

- Greater numbers of families coming from regions of the world in which their native language may not be a written language (e.g., only in the last 20 years did Hmong become a written language)
- More families coming from agrarian rather than urban societies
- More families coming to America to flee war in their native lands
- Greater numbers of families in which support systems differ from traditional American families (e.g., the role of folk healers)

The implications of these challenges imply different strategies when reaching out to families. Communication becomes a crucial issue when the arrival English of these families is minimal. Helping parents to understand how the American educational system functions and what programs are available to their children (bilingual, English as a Second Language or ESL, etc.) is becoming an increasingly important issue for schools. In addition, many of these immigrant children and their family members may be scarred emotionally and physically from the wars in their homelands. If the support systems for these families are indeed different from the traditional two-parent family, what impact will this have on school-family-community relations?

For a variety of reasons, traditional kinds of parent involvement may be problematic for many families. Single-parent families may find it difficult to get child care in order to attend a parent conference; they may work hours that are inconvenient for attending a school meeting. Also, they may lack transportation to the school. This is especially true when children attend nonneighborhood schools. Understanding a language is another potential obstacle for attending school conferences. Are translators available for meetings with non-English-speaking families? Furthermore, many parents come from cultures where parental involvement in schools is minimal.

Formulating a New Concept of Family
The village raises the child. (African proverb)

Given the many changes in American society today, it is time for schools to redefine the term *family.* The current definition of family, individuals who are related by marriage or adoption, is no longer typical of the living arrangements of many people in our society. Economic, social, and cultural influences are forcing schools to reach out to an extended family. This extended family may be composed of a variety of people, depending on the child and his or her background. Typically, we think of parents as playing a crucial role in raising children. We must expand our definition to consider the roles of grandparents, older siblings, aunts, uncles, and other blood or marriage relatives. In addition to these family members, the extended family comprises a variety of people representing numerous support systems, including religious institutions, social clubs, folk healers, teachers, godparents, child-care workers, social service agency personnel, family friends, relatives, and so on.

It is vital for school personnel to recognize that for many children from different cultural backgrounds the family encompasses not only those tied to it through kinship. A variety of people play important roles in supporting children as they pass through our schools. Reaching out to these extended families, whether they are blood relatives or not, must be the new arena for schools.

Creating a New Paradigm for Family Involvement

Traditionally, when we think of parent involvement in schools, what comes to mind is parents doing such things as attending open house, parent conferences, individualized education plan (IEP) meetings, school plays, concerts, field days, science fairs or award ceremonies; volunteering to help in a classroom or a library; asking how to better help his or her child at home; responding to a message from school; helping the Parent-Teacher Association/ Organization (PTA/O) at a bake sale; and so on. Many of these rituals, ceremonies, and roles for parents have changed very little in the past 100 years. Conventionalized school activities that have been institutionalized to involve parents in limited ways tend to relegate all the power to the institution and have usually ignored the needs of groups, particularly those families with a different language who are unfamiliar with the school's expectations.

Many educators continue to believe that schools need to increase this role for parents, even though most parents cannot, and do not, participate at the school building. We repeatedly hear the same complaints from educators: "Parents don't really care about their children." "We hardly ever get a large number of parents to come to open house." "The parents who do come are not necessarily the ones we need to see." "We either have parents we never see, or it's the same ones trying to control what we do." "(Racial/ethnic group's name) don't value education."

There are a variety of reasons why many families are not, or do not appear to be, involved in their child's schooling. If we continue to think of family involvement only in traditional ways (attending open house, volunteering in school, etc.), then there are many families who will never be "involved." Instead, by redefining *family* and *involvement*, making both terms more inclusive, we can look at other critical issues affecting involvement such as time, cultural differences, economic factors, and so on.

Thus we need to broaden our definition of parental involvement. Instead of using the term *parent involvement*, we will use the term *family involvement* because of the changing definition of family. When we think of family, we usually envision the school-child-family tie. However, family involvement begins with the family and the child. Therefore, the goals for schools should be to maximize the number of families actively involved in their children's education.

The empowerment of families is based on certain social, cultural, and political assumptions. School personnel should have an understanding of the history of a given community or group, including the language, values, and traditions associated with role allocations. This information is essential in determining appropriate strategies for reducing possible inequality.

Child-rearing practices at home are sociocultural skills that are learned through mediating structures that interlink. These structures include the family, the church, the school, the neighborhood, and the parents' workplace. These undergirding principles of socialization allow us to understand how families develop strengths and how these strengths need to be recognized by educators.

Relying on simple solutions to explain lack of achievement deflects attention away from the schools' responsibility to develop effective programs for students from underrepresented groups. Among the issues that must be taken into account in realistically addressing student lack of achievement are cultural group identity, parents' knowledge background, the family's socioeconomic conditions, and the parents' understanding about the U.S. educational system and the particular school. Discussion and consideration of these issues will help foster effective community linkages that enhance school opportunities for students and their families.

There are different challenges for educators, depending on the socioeconomic status (SES) of the family. The challenge for educators in low SES communities is to build up levels of involvement in schooling; whereas teachers in most suburban communities with upper- and middle-class families are likely to enjoy parental participation but confront problems with limiting and controlling parent behavior.

The important issue to remember is that parents are not the problem. Most times, the problem is structural. It is crucial to remember that families and schools play complementary roles in the task of bringing children into adulthood.

Reaching out to extended families will be a major task for school administrators. Public relations methods will need to include approaches that are not traditionally used in schools because the demands placed on schools by the changing populations will require closer ties between families and school. But the number of hard-to-reach families is much smaller than many believe. In reality, schools have tended to use the same public relations methods to involve or inform parents. Many of these methods worked in the past (some did not and we continued to use them anyway), but they are not effective today given the changes in society, families, and cultural differences.

Categories of Family Involvement

Epstein (1992) discusses five types of parental involvement in their child's education: parenting, communicating, volunteering, learning at home, and representing other parents. As discussed earlier, referring to this involvement as parent involvement is limiting; thus we are adapting Epstein's five categories to include the involvement of the extended family.

Parenting

Parenting refers to helping families to establish environments that are conducive to learning. School administrators and other personnel must be seen as advocates for children. They can help to locate needed community social services. For example, they can assist parents in devising ways to attend to family matters while not keeping children home from school. In some families, the only speaker of English is the school-age child who must be absent from school because he or she needs to translate for the family in business matters. If school personnel help families with these problems, then families can increase their involvement in school-related issues.

Schools should encourage families to rely on their cultural values. This might be through religious observance; important family rites and rituals; or deep-seated values such as responsibilities, respect for elders, or high academic aspirations. Children should basically like their parents and show respect for them even though they may see their parents as too strict and old-fashioned.

Listed below are some questions the school might examine:

- What relationships do family members have with the child?
- Does the family maintain a high level of communication?
- Are parents and other family members loving and supportive?
- Does the family try to create a stress-free home environment?
- Are tasks assigned to the child at home?
- Do family members encourage the child to complete tasks?
- Does the family stress the importance of going to school?
- What skills has the child been taught by family members?
- Does the child basically like his or her family members?
- Does the child respect them?
- Are family members models of strength and resilience?

When working with racially and/or ethnically diverse families, it is crucial to consider a variety of other aspects unique to ethnically diverse families. We suggest exploring the following questions:

- What natural support systems exist for the culture? (e.g., extended family, folk healers, institutions, social clubs)
- What language(s) are spoken in the home?

- Do family members read and write in those languages?
- How long has the family been residing in the United States?
- What was their arrival level of English?
- For how many generations has this cultural group resided in this community?
- How large is this cultural group?
- Are there community organizations with ties to this group?
- How, if at all, are family members related?
- What role(s) does the child play in this family? (gender? oldest sibling? youngest?)
- What are the expectations of the family regarding the child? (e.g., taking care of siblings, working part-time)
- What religion, if any, does the family practice?
- What is their frequency of attendance and importance of involvement?
- Are there special religious holidays celebrated by the family?
- Do their children have any dietary restrictions associated with religious practices?
- Does the child follow any daily religious rituals?

Communicating

Communicating includes the many ways schools reach out to enhance communication between the school and home. These communications may be written, oral, and/or visual. School personnel should do everything possible to ensure that all communications are two-way. The literature tells us that students in schools that maintain frequent contact with their communities outperform those in other schools, and positive effects persist past short-term reliance on native language and culture that seem to promote academic success. The school might use the following questions in examining its practices:

- In what ways does the school communicate information to families?
- How does the school know if communications were received?

- How does the school encourage the family to monitor the child's progress?
- How often do teachers communicate with the family? What types of communication do they have? (phone, mail, in person)
- Have teachers met with family members early on in the school year?
- Does the family understand this program?

Suggestions for enhancing school-family communications with ethnically diverse parents include the following:

- Translate newsletters, classroom letters, parent memos, report cards, and handbooks into appropriate languages.
- Make home visits by school personnel (accompanied by translators if necessary).
- Create new ceremonies and rituals such as annual international dinners/ethnic fairs.
- Address letters with the salutation, "Dear Family Member."
- Start group meetings with teachers and/or administrators inside or outside school.
- Loan videotapes of typical classes or special projects to families with a voice-over in other languages.
- Provide translators for parent-teacher meetings.
- Invite parents and other community members who represent cultural groups in the school as guest speakers.
- Form partnerships with local businesses to allow family members to have release time from work without losing pay to make school visits.
- Identify key informants from each cultural group who can relate information about the school to members of that group.
- Find ways to provide transportation to school functions for those families that require it (perhaps these key informants can be of assistance).
- Schedule school events at staggered times so families can attend when possible.

- Be aware of the holidays families celebrate so that meetings and school programs do not conflict with religious or ethnic celebrations.

When working with ethnically diverse families, it is crucial to consider a variety of other aspects that are unique to their cultures. For example, according to Yao (1988), because many Asian immigrants tend to be reserved, school personnel need to take the initiative for activities. Schools need to use interpreters to provide seminars so parents can become familiar with basic features of the school system, such as educational services and programs, extracurricular activities, general school policy and facilities, and procedures and policies for assessment and evaluation. School personnel should monitor the language they use. First, they should emphasize the child's strengths, then problems or weaknesses can be introduced. Establishing a trusting relationship with children and their families should be a priority before the teacher begins to explore ways to assess children's behavior. Teachers must clearly explain the remediation plan. Carefully choosing words is crucial. Yao suggests substituting the word *disinterested* for *lazy*; *unfamiliar with American customs* for *rude*; and *reserved* for *passive.*

Teachers should be familiar with symbols that may have negative connotations in the cultures represented by the children in their classrooms. Families from certain Native American tribes, Vietnam, and several other Asian cultures might be surprised when their child receives a graduation card with an owl on it. In their culture an owl may be an omen that something bad is about to occur. It can even mean death in some cultures. Similarly, the color white is a symbol of the dead in some cultures, whereas in the United States it has been traditional to wear black to a funeral.

Nonverbal language plays a critical role in communication. Problems between families and school personnel may result in personnel who are not trained to understand some of these differences. People in some cultures show respect by avoiding eye contact. Even laughter might be a sign of nervousness rather than an expression of amusement. In many cultures personal distance (proxemics) is closer than in the United States. This might result in a teacher stepping back from a child or a family member during conversation. The teacher infers that the person is invading his or her territory, thus he or she retreats. Members of the other culture might infer that the teacher is trying to get way from them or does not like them. The crucial point to remember is that a trusting relationship between school personnel and the family is the key to the family's involvement in the education of the child.

Volunteering

Volunteering involves recruiting and organizing parents to help in school. Teachers and administrators express the need to have parents in the schools, but all too often the reality is that they need parents only in ways defined by the school; thus the school personnel hold the power while the needs of the families may not be explored. Many educators have not seen the value of involving parents on a continuous basis to prevent conflict and problems with children. Rather, parents are usually brought in when a problem exists. To have well-informed parents who will know how to work along with the teacher, and to open lines of communication, school personnel must view the effort as cost-effective and fund parent education as well as parent-teacher activities.

Teachers in inner cities report that they want all parents to perform helpful activities in the elementary and middle grades. But few schools have programs to help parents understand how to conduct these activities with their children at different grade levels. Teachers at all grade levels tend to blame parents for their low level of involvement. Yet other teachers—sometimes in the same schools—successfully involve similar parents in their children's education as part of regular teaching practices. Districts should consider K-12 parent education programs that might include English-language classes, conflict resolution seminars, and workshops with topics such as communicating with children and cross-cultural differences. Questions for school personnel to discuss might include the following:

- How are families involved in the school itself?

- How frequent is participation?
- Do family members play a role in school decision making?
- Do families feel they are having an impact on the school?
- Does the school have a family-advisory council or other built-in mechanisms for their input?

Again, when working with ethnically diverse families, it is crucial to consider a variety of other aspects unique to ethnically diverse families.

Listed below are some suggestions:

- Invite adult family members to school to discuss traditions, customs, and cultural mores.
- Use adults from various cultural groups as role models to break stereotypes of cultural groups.
- Have a "Parents' Corner" of the school newsletter and encourage parents to contribute to it either through writing a letter themselves or being interviewed by parent volunteers.

Helping Families Assist Children Outside School

A fourth way to promote involvement is helping families to assist children in learning outside the school. Research on parental/family assistance at home has important consequences for children's achievement, school adaptability, classroom behavior, and attendance. In addition, we know that extra learning time at home for lower elementary students produces gains in reading scores that are equivalent to those made by students under more expensive pullout programs in schools. We know that students at all grade levels are likely to benefit from family involvement.

Schools must help families to be proud of their children and show how they can demonstrate it. Families should have high expectations of their children. They should not tend to focus on grades, but they should use them as a measure of the child's efforts. If they believe the child can do better, they should be quick to tell him or her. Schools should foster the idea that children are a source of hope for families.

Questions school personnel need to ask include the following:

- Does the family stress the importance of going to school and college?
- Are these constant themes in the home?
- Does the family provide support by monitoring homework?
- Do they have expectations that the child will complete it?
- Do they ask about school frequently?
- Do they ensure that their children get to school?
- Is the child read to?

When working with culturally diverse families it is crucial to consider a variety of other aspects unique for their backgrounds. Listed below are some suggestions:

- Have families read to their children in the language in which they are most comfortable reading.
- Be sure families try to find a quiet space for children to complete their homework. (This may be the school in the evening, the local library, etc.)
- Encourage families to continue any oral traditions they may have for storytelling.

Representing Other Parents

The final category, representing other parents, refers to recruiting and training parent leaders so they can act as parent advocates. Traditionally, PTOs or PTAs have played an important role in many schools. However, all too often attendance is poor, with the same parents involved in activities. If the definition of parental involvement is expanded to family involvement as discussed earlier, then there are many implications for expanding parent-teacher organizations. Perhaps these organizations need to reach out to the extended family as well. It is important to remember that parents and family members do get more involved when schools give them some direction.

Listed below are some suggestions:

- Identify key informants from various cultural groups to help you keep all families informed.
- Work with the PTO or PTA in ensuring that the organization reaches out to all the school's cultural groups.
- Identify and collaborate with key cultural organizations in the community (National Association for the Advancement of Colored People or NAACP, League of United Latin-American Citizens or LULAC, etc.)

Epstein's five categories of parental involvement have been expanded here to include family involvement containing issues of cultural diversity. If our goal is to increase the number of families actively involved in their children's education, then welcoming the entire extended family and being cognizant of cultural factors will help educators to attain this goal.

Schools as Caring Communities

Knowing the Community

Once school personnel realize the importance of joining together with extended families, they will begin to look at the cultural and language resources they have in these adults rather than focusing on their lack of English-language proficiency as a deficit. As key informants in the community are sought out and nurtured, a vast resource will begin to open up to school personnel. School administrators need to tap these resources as much as possible.

To explore the community, school personnel will need to find out what organizations or institutions, as well as people and issues, are the lifeblood of that community. The school administrator needs to develop an entrée plan that will provide the needed information so they can facilitate collaborative efforts.

Collaborating and Forming Partnerships

Institutions and organizations in the community refer to agencies offering social services, both private and public; social clubs; religious associations; youth groups; volunteer agencies; school-related organizations and groups, both formal and informal; the chamber of commerce; Rotary Club; volunteer fire fighters; YWCA/YMCA; summer camps; and so on. All of these entities need to be tied to schools: some loosely tied and others more tightly coupled. In addition, ethnic groups may have ties to social clubs, folk healers, merchants, herbalists, religious personnel, and so on.

A potentially powerful institution in every community that can help connect the school and the community is the local library. After school, on weekends, and during school vacations, libraries can offer a wide variety of programs to schoolchildren as well as their families. They can serve as community centers offering adults and children tutoring, and meeting rooms can be available for groups to use. These library community centers could schedule seminars, workshops, field trips, and so on. Depending on the ethnic groups located in the community, the library can also have book, video, and film collections in several languages. Charging minimal fees, these library community centers might offer the use of photocopiers; notary services; rental of computers, typewriters, camcorders, and cameras; shut-in service; voter registration service; purchase of postage stamps; baby-sitting; and so on. The possibilities are enormous. If communities had such centers, they would complement school programs. Rather than thinking of schools as the only places that can offer these additional services by expanding their hours, the responsibilities can be shared by a variety of organizations.

Questions school personnel will need to explore include the following:

- What organizations are located in the school's community?
- What social service agencies serve the community?

- Who are the key people in those organizations?
- What populations do they serve?
- What resources do they have available?
- How might the school and the organization collaborate to provide a service?
- What ethnic groups are located in the community?
- What affiliations do these ethnic groups have with these and other organizations?
- Who are the leaders of these ethnic communities?

By exploring the above questions, administrators will better understand the community. By using computer technology, schools can build a database of these organizations that can be regularly updated. Because a major focus of TQE is on the prevention of problems, knowing the potential of the school's community and the importance of forging strong ties with its organizations is a crucial step toward preventing problems for children and their families.

Welcoming Families to Schools

William Purkey and Paula Stanley introduced the concept of invitational education. TQE and invitational education complement one another because both focus on "the customer." As the authors have explained,

> Invitational education proposes that people are able, valuable, and responsible and should be treated accordingly. . . .
> It proposes that individuals possess relatively untapped potential. . . . This potential can be realized through the places, policies, and programs that are specifically designed to facilitate human development, and through people [who] are intentionally inviting with themselves and others, personally and professionally. (Purkey & Stanley, 1991, p. 15)

The challenge for educators is to ensure that schools are intentionally inviting (rather than disinviting) places for children, their families, and the community.

Questions to consider include the following:

- Is the name of the school identifiable from the street?
- Can a visitor recognize the main entrance?
- Is there easy access to parking?
- Is the school's neighborhood a safe place for visitors to enter?
- Are there physical barriers to entering the school (e.g., locked main entrance doors)?
- Are visitors greeted courteously?
- Are translators available if necessary?
- Are school brochures and other materials translated into the languages found in the community?
- Are there professional staff members who speak these languages?

New Roles for Schools: Rebuilding Sociocultural Capital

The theory of overlapping spheres of influence is designed to encourage research on the effects of specific connections of schools and families on children. Because the school's focus is on helping children to reach their potential, Figure 5.2 shows the overlap of the influences of schools, communities, and families—the village—in nurturing children. Through what Freire (1970) calls *praxis*, which is reflection with action in the pursuit of social change, educators can seek innovative ways to help rebuild the sociocultural capital in communities and families in which it was lost or never nurtured. This sociocultural capital can be drawn on in order to help the child. The capital held by people (parents, older siblings, grandparents, other relatives, family friends, educators, community members, etc.) resides in the strength of social relationships and cultural values that allows them to call on the

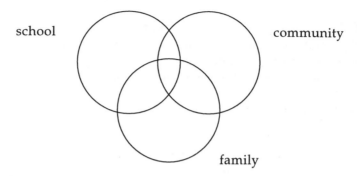

Figure 5.2. Sociocultural Capital

resources of others. The family's knowledge, confidence, competence, and actions about their children's education make up these skills. Sometimes educators hold the misbelief that the mere presence of adults in the home assures that capital exists. Through building strong relationships with families and the community, educators can help link the resources with the capital.

Thus the school has three major roles to play with families: (a) explore what sociocultural capital exists in the family; (b) rebuild it where it is weak; and (c) forge links among the school, family, and community to strengthen resources for children.

A school with extensive sociocultural capital in the community is one in which families join to set standards of behavior and dress for their children, to make rules that are similar among families, and to provide support for their own and each other's children. The change must come not in substituting for families but in facilitating those actions of the family that can aid most the joint task of family, community, and school in bringing children into adulthood. Thus schools must devise ways to replenish the supply of capital on which youngsters can draw.

Listed below are ideas to consider for rebuilding sociocultural capital:

- Cut back on some of the demands on families.
- Prioritize the school's goals for families.
- Broaden the strategies to realize these goals.

- Link families with community agencies.
- Include ethnic/racial community organizations in school activities.
- Provide districtwide family education programs from preschool through high school.
- Consider the extended family as a true asset and tap all members' potential resources.
- Ensure that the school is a welcoming environment for family and community members.
- Foster links with the community by changing nonproductive school rituals and ceremonies.
- Reflect on current school rituals and ceremonies. Who do they involve? What new ties can be made to the family and community through different rituals and ceremonies? How can the school tie the family and the community's cultural diversity to these rituals and ceremonies?

The barriers to the full participation of families and communities in schools can be removed with training, encouragement, and resources that ensure equal access.

Key Terms and Concepts

Bilingual education. Instruction in two languages and the use of those two languages as mediums of instruction for any part of or all the school curriculum.

ESL. English as a Second Language. Instruction in the English language in ways that assist nonnative speakers of English to acquire proficiency in English.

Extended family. In this chapter this refers to related and unrelated persons who are involved with the upbringing of a child.

Family. A family traditionally consists of two or more people who are related by blood, marriage, or adoption who reside together in a household.

Household. Families and households differ in that households include related family members and all unrelated persons (e.g., foster children, family friends, etc.).

LEP. Limited English proficient. Lacking proficiency in the English language.

Praxis. Freire's term for the process of connecting reflection with action in the pursuit of knowledge and social change.

SES. Socioeconomic status.

Single-parent family. This refers to a male or a female with no spouse present who resides with other relatives. Not all single-parent families have children.

Sociocultural capital. This refers to the collective social skills and cultural mores, beliefs, and traditions that can be drawn upon (in this case from the extended family, the school, and the community) in helping the child.

References

Epstein, J. L. (1992, March 25-26) *Theory to practice: School and family partnerships for school improvement and student success.* Paper presented at the National Education Conference, Los Angeles.

Freire, P. (1970). *Pedagogy of the oppressed.* New York: Seabury.

Kellogg, J. B. (1988, November). Forces of change. *Phi Delta Kappan.* p. 199-204.

Outtz, J. H. (1993). *The demographics of American families.* Washington, DC: Institute for Educational Leadership.

Purkey, W. W., & Stanley, P. H. (1991). *Invitational teaching, learning, and living.* Washington, DC: National Education Association.

Yao, E. L. (1988, November). Working effectively with Asian immigrant parents. *Phi Delta Kappan,* pp. 223-225.

✧ **6** ✧

Sustaining a Multicultural Ethos

Changing Mind-sets

The previous chapters have suggested that the history of education is checkered with inequities and inconsistencies in quality education for *all children*. Indeed, schools have historically been organized in ways that maintain the status quo and facilitate monocultural ideals. Because this prevailing structure cannot continue, educational organizations need to reorganize themselves in order to achieve a better match with an emerging multicultural ethos. Building institutional support for a multicultural perspective in schools, however, will require a fundamental shift in patterns of thinking: from compartmentalized and bureaucratic mind-sets to more interdependent and systemic dimensions. As in nature, where new biological forms constantly emerge as old ones dissolve, a new educational ecology is needed to foster a healthy climate for the present social context of schools.

The metaphor of ecology is useful in describing the interconnection between the educational culture and the environment. Ecology suggests interdependence and a way of understanding the interconnection of our lives and our actions to the environment. This perspective suggests the need for an increased awareness of how our actions and thoughts directly influence schools. Understanding interdependence requires that we consider for example, patterns of relationships, communication, language, and culture. How do we relate to parents? How do teachers interact with children? What is being taught? How does the administrator communicate to the staff or the community? How are decisions made? Are the communities involved? Are there teachers who speak a second language? What cultures are represented in the community? These, as well as other considerations suggested in previous chapters, take into account the patterns and interrelationships between all members of a school community. From an educational ecology perspective, all levels of the educational process are involved. Only the complexity will vary.

Challenging Mental Models

To counter prevailing (or unproductive) patterns of thought, we must begin by asking the question, How can the quality of education be improved for all children? This question is essential because it implies a review of mental models that guide everyday work life in schools.

Mental models are ingrained assumptions, ideas, and generalizations that influence how we understand the world around us and our actions. Mental models can shape our perceptions and determine how we make sense of the world. Senge (1990a) describes mental models as

> simple generalizations such as "people are untrustworthy," or they can be complex theories, such as my assumptions about why members of my family interact as they do. But what is most important to grasp is that mental models are active—they shape how we act. If we believe people are untrustworthy, we act differently from the way we would if we believed they were trustworthy. (p. 175)

Mental models are powerful in that they affect what we do. Educators can begin to improve the quality of education for *all children* by reflecting on what has been done in the past.

The first step toward galvanizing support for a multicultural ethos is to expose the mental models and practices that accompany them. The best way to do this is to develop abilities that help us to examine our worldview. Senge (1990a) has suggested some skills to keep in mind:

1. Slow down our thinking. Beware of leaping from first observations into generalizations.
2. Articulate what we normally do not say. Face the problem head-on.
3. Be honest and willing to expose limitations in our own thinking.
4. Recognize and change the gap between what we say and what we do.

Educators must be willing to engage in a dynamic form of self-evaluation that calls attention to preconceived notions regarding multicultural education. Total Quality Education is ideally suited to this endeavor because it is fundamentally an improvement-based process.

Educators are notorious for attempting to change specific elements of education without examining the larger perspective.

In educational reform movements, only separate pieces of the puzzle are confronted—such as teacher pay practices, supervisory evaluations, or student assessments—without addressing the entire "ecology" of the school organization. This important oversight encourages changes that lack consistency, purpose, and constancy of meaning. Total Quality Education, on the other hand, suggests that improving a school's organization and administration will require a "holistic" focus, where decision makers examine the totality of education and the interdependence of its parts. This is the first step toward altering one's perception of schooling and facilitating institutionalized support for a multicultural ethos.

The second question we need to ask is, What is the true purpose of the educational system? A major theme of TQE is the need for all individuals to maintain constancy of purpose and beliefs. To our mind, a central purpose of education is to facilitate students' pleasure in learning and promote the desire to continue the process. One accompanying belief is that *all* students are capable of finding joy in learning and furthering their discoveries. Staying focused on these core purposes and beliefs is vital to establishing a constant purpose of quality learning in multicultural settings.

Creative Tension

A third question for consideration is, How can purposes and beliefs related to multicultural education be articulated throughout an organization? Senge's (1990b) principle of creative tension (see chapter 3) advances the notion that leaders should focus on transforming current reality and articulating a new vision. This might be a useful tool for administrators who are interested in negotiating new ideas for multicultural education. Senge (1990b) explains:

> Creative tension comes from seeing clearly where we want to be, our "vision," and telling the truth about where we are, our current reality. (p. 9)

A further elaboration of this point was made by Dr. Martin Luther King, Jr. (1986), who once said,

> Just as Socrates felt that it was necessary to create a tension in the mind, so that individuals could rise from bondage of myths and half truths . . . so must we . . . create the kind of tension in society that will help men rise from the dark depths of prejudice and racism. (p. 52)

Hence a school administrator might, for example, stage a panel discussion in a faculty meeting where divergent views and ideas about "realities" (what is) as opposed to "visions" (what should be) can be expressed.

Without a guiding vision of what we want for children in a culturally diverse school world, educators will continue to stumble through old habits and patterns that foster cynicism and frustration. But having a vision, yet failing to understand the nature of reality, encourages a setting in which the energy and drive needed for creativity and change will dissipate. As Jonathan

Kozol's (1991) *Savage Inequalities* aptly documents, existing resource inequities and differential treatment of students highlight the broad gap between what we say and what we do.

If administrators are to reconceptualize how a school vision can improve learning in culturally diverse classrooms, a fundamental shift in thinking is required. The creative-tension principle suggests that administrators often focus and spend energy on visions for change as a means of avoiding current reality. However, the creative-tension orientation also teaches us that "an accurate picture of current reality is just as important as a compelling picture of the desired future" (Senge, 1990b, p. 12). School administrators who ignore current reality are not often inclined to evaluate current school policies or classroom practices until obvious problems arise. Consequently, changes in policies and work practices that are implemented tend to be quick fixes as opposed to long-term solutions. Teachers and administrators who implement them may quickly run out of steam. As Senge (1990b) notes, "The energy for change comes from the vision, from what we want to create, juxtaposed with current reality" (p. 9).

Administrators who seek to change school organizations through creative tension focus primarily on central purposes and beliefs for schooling (as opposed to what is *not* wanted). In this context, altering current reality "comes from holding a picture of what might be that is more important to people than what is" (Senge, 1990b, p. 9).

Below is a checklist that administrators can use to assess the development of a school culture that supports and sustains a multicultural ethos.

Please rate the items on the following scale: 1 = *strongly agree*; 2 = *agree*; 3 = *disagree*; 4 = *strongly disagree*

_____ 1. School personnel have expressed an interest in enhancing student learning by using approaches that are sensitive and relevant to students' sociocultural background and experiences.

(continued)

_____ 2. During the past year, faculty and administrators have tried to create new and different learning opportunities to develop student's social, academic, and/or personal skills.

If any changes have been implemented, please list them here:

      a.

      b.

      c.

_____ 3. Teachers and administrators in this school often presume that cultural and language differences inhibit scholarly work.

_____ 4. Faculty in this school demonstrate a desire to expand the definition of parent involvement, increase communication with parents, and use the strengths and resources parents possess in their culture and language.

_____ 5. Teachers perceive that minority parents speak in other languages and are thus unable to support and provide skills that strengthen academic learning at home.

Whereas items 1, 2, and 4 focus on the vision and the possible goals of school faculty (what we want), items 3 and 5 deal more with possible reality (what we do not want). If you agreed with both the vision and reality statements, then a mismatch may exist in your school between vision and reality. For example, although teachers may express a desire to view student diversity as an advantage in their instruction, in reality they may believe that diversity inhibits student scholarship.

In practice, school personnel often focus most of their energy on what is not wanted (reality) as opposed to what is (vision). A subtle alteration in perspective—toward a focus on what *is* wanted carefully weighed against reality—is important for administra-

	Individual	Organization
Self-maintaining	Self-aware	Goals and activities are shared
Self-renewing	Reflection-in-action	Respond to new situations and seek continuous improvement
Self-transcending	New perspective; able to change old assumptions	Reconstruction; redesign

Figure 6.1. Characteristics of Healthy Schools

tors who want to be effective in multicultural settings. It requires a shift in old thinking patterns (i.e., focusing on what we do not want). The old pattern of thinking takes away time, energy, and perhaps most important, derails purpose.

Self-Maintaining, Self-Renewing, and Self-Transcending Schools

Thus far this chapter has tried to emphasize that schools must build an institutional ethos that sustains a multicultural emphasis. However, valuing diversity alone is an insufficient condition for change. Organizations must also have the capability to be self-maintaining, self-renewing, and self-transcending (Capra, 1989; see Figure 6.1).

Self-maintaining means that organizational members are self-aware: Perceptions about work activities and goals are shared. Individual awareness is included here. Both the organization and the individuals are aware of the collective meanings that help bind an organization together. Awareness generated by self-maintaining necessitates that we continue to use and improve our perceptions about work. In this way we can refine, adapt, and simplify our conception of reorganization and methodological understanding of multiculturalism. For example, the act of designing an instructional program that is responsive to the multicultural needs of the students requires an ongoing and shared understanding of the value of diversity by teachers, students, community, and administration.

To understand the importance of shared meaning and goals, systemic human connections and interactions that occur in educational organizations are key to TQE and the pursuit of the invisible processes that promote quality. According to TQE, discovering the individual and his or her connection to the school is the exact condition necessary for instilling a climate of quality that will improve all forms and processes of the organization. In organizations that are self-maintaining the educational goals and activities are shared.

Self-renewal means that organizational participants are able to respond to new situations. To develop this type of competency, organizational professionals must use their own inner abilities to navigate waters that are unique, uncertain, and rife with conflict. These competencies do not necessarily rely on facts or conscious knowledge that direct one's actions. Rather, professionals seem to be relying on an inner knowingness that has defied objective description (Martinez, 1989). Polanyi (1969) described this inner knowingness, or knowing more than one can say, as tacit knowledge. Similarly, TQE focuses on process and facilitation of constant improvement of the system that can be applied to the self as well as the institution.

The TQE approach to improvement is not a quick fix. It calls for a fundamental change of operation that encourages a self-renewing process. An example of self-renewal would be the ability of a school administrator to respond differently to the fragmented day-to-day tasks of school administration. For example, Martinez (1989) cited the case of a principal who recreated an environment at a school in a Native American community that was being strangled by bureaucratic and budgetary limitations. Facing adversity required risk taking and reflection on the part of the principal. Martinez (1989) describes the experience:

Awareness of both inner and outer voices is the key here.
One should be spontaneous in exploring possibilities. Ideas
and problem solutions do not come on "cue"; rather, they
emerge from inner knowledge. Noticing, being, creating,
and exploring self offer to the principal infinite possibilities. (p. 93)

In multicultural and diverse settings, reshaping one's thinking—that is, reflecting on actions in order to discover an action
that will make a difference—is what Schön (1983, 1987) refers to
as *reflection-in-action*.

In organizations that are capable of renewing themselves, members have the capacity to constantly "reflect-in-action." Schön
(1983, 1987) describes this capacity as follows:

Reflection-in-action has a critical function, to question the
assumptional structure of knowing-in-action. We think
critically about the thinking that got us into this fix or this
opportunity; and we may, in the process, restructure strategies of action, understandings of phenomena, or ways of
framing problems. . . . Reflection gives rise to on-the-spot
experiment . . . it may work, again in the sense of yielding
intended results, or it may produce surprises that call for
further reflection and experiment. (p. 28)

Self-transcending means that organizational participants are able
to engage in ongoing learning processes and to transfer knowledge from one experience to the next. Learning becomes a resyn-
thesis of prior analytic (or reflection-in-action) accomplishments.
From this experience, individuals are able to change their fundamental assumptions and perceptions about the purposes of multicultural
education and increase their sensitivity to, and recognition of, the
diversity of groups in our society. At the heart of this notion is the
TQE emphasis on continuous improvement. The concept of quality and improvement is central to self-transformation, and trans-
formation is everyone's job.

For example, Nieto (1992) points out that many schools operate according to a tolerance model, where it is assumed that diversity is automatically accounted for by including some aspect of culture in a curriculum unit, such as Black History Month, or having a "multicultural teacher." On the other hand, Nieto's (1992) affirmation model would stress that multicultural strategies pervade the curriculum and consciousness of all school members. From this perspective, everyone would take responsibility for multicultural education. Self-transcendence means that a school is capable of moving from a tolerance model to an affirmation model.

In organizations that are capable of transcending themselves, opportunities are provided for the development of individuals within the organization. Self-transcending organizations are learning organizations. The organization achieves this by calling on the totality of its membership. All members of the educational community thus work together to define and recreate practice.

The self-transcending educational organization should possess the following characteristics:

1. The organization constantly responds to changes because it is fundamentally interconnected to the external world.
2. Individual members redefine their purpose as the organization shifts.
3. Knowledge that is earned through the experience of change is applied by the total community to achieve an ongoing learning cycle.
4. Individual members seek out knowledge to improve practice.

Each of these characteristics facilitate the ongoing reconstruction and redesign of multiculturalism into a new perspective.

The reconstruction of a multicultural perspective thus proceeds in an evolutionary manner. The principle of evolution states that successful organisms are those that have transcended the self in response to external change, thus surviving where others fail. It is through redesign from within that the multicultural ethos can sustain itself into the future.

Key Terms and Concepts

Creative tension. Senge's term for describing the juxtaposition of vision (what we want) and a clear picture of current reality (where we are relative to what we want).

Educational ecology. This refers to the interconnection between the educational culture and the environment.

Mental models. Senge's term for ingrained assumptions, ideas, and generalizations that influence how we understand the world around us and how it affects our behavior.

Multicultural ethos. Multicultural ethos embraces multicultural education as a basic framework for the creation of values that guide an educational institution.

Self-maintaining. This refers to the individual's ability to be self-aware in relation to the shared meaning and goals of an educational organization.

Self-renewal. This refers to the individual's ability to reflect on actions in order to discover what will make a difference. It is the process of seeking continuous improvement.

Self-transcending. This refers to the individual's ability to change his or her fundamental assumptions about the world.

References

Capra, B. (Director). (1989). *Mindwalk* [Film]. Hollywood, CA: Atlas Production Company.

King, M. L., Jr. (1964). Letter from Birmingham jail. In M.L. King, Jr. (Ed.), *Why we can't wait* (pp.77-100). New York: Harper & Row.

Kozol, J. (1991). *Savage inequalities.* New York: Crown.

Martinez, L. (1989). *Principal as artist: A model for transforming a school community.* Unpublished doctoral dissertation, Vanderbilt University.

Nieto, S. (1992). *Affirming diversity: The sociopolitical context of multicultural education.* New York: Longman.

Polanyi, M. (1969). *Knowing and being.* Chicago: University of Chicago Press.

Schön, D. A. (1983). *The reflective practitioner: How professionals think in action.* New York: Basic Books.

Schön, D. A. (1987). *Educating the reflective practitioner.* San Francisco: Jossey-Bass.

Senge, P. M. (1990a). *The fifth discipline: The art & practice of the learning organization.* New York: Doubleday.

Senge, P. M. (1990b). The leader's review new work: Building learning organizations. *Sloan Management Review, 32,* 7-23.

✧ 7 ✧

Total Quality Leadership:
New Skills for a Changing Paradigm

*The essential activity for keeping our paradigm current is persist-
ent questioning.*

(PASCAL, 1990, p. 14)

In this book we have raised many questions that we hope will help
to keep the school administrator's paradigm current with regard
to the issues and challenges of cultural diversity. This chapter
outlines six behaviors on the part of school leaders that will enable
them to accomplish the goals of TQE through the lenses of awareness of, and sensitivity to, cultural diversity. We conclude the
chapter with a metaphor—that of a jalapeño in a candy jar—to
emphasize the affirming of cultural diversity.

Modeling Behavior

Matching behaviors to words is a critical aspect of school
leadership; it is the isomorphic relation that needs to exist between espoused theory and theory in use. For example, if a school
administrator espouses the belief that discrimination and racism
cannot be a part of the school community, but fails to address
structural inequities, he or she is not matching espoused theory
with behavior. Thus the message to the school community is
unclear, misunderstood, and conflicts with the vision being espoused by the leader. Matching espoused theory and theory in use
are essential to modeling.

Key questions for TQE leaders are the following:

- Do my words and behaviors match my beliefs and values?
- What reflection and inquiry strategies can I use to determine if I model my espoused theory?

Cultivating a Collaborative School Culture

School culture includes the shared beliefs, values, and mores of the school. School administrators need to cultivate a genuine ethos of collaboration in order to help the school community become a learning community. This involves welcoming diverse perspectives and voices so this diversity can enhance the democracy of the school community. Because a strong school culture is needed for school improvement efforts, the challenge for the administrator is to harness the intellectual capital of all staff members to help tie the community together. Changing a school's culture takes time and persistence, and as Warren Bennis (1990) has written, "Leaders need passion, energy and focus."

Key questions for TQE leaders are the following:

- How can I determine if this school has a true ethos of collaboration?
- In what ways can I strengthen the school culture so that diverse perspectives are given voice?

Embracing a Vision

Once the school administrator understands the culture of a school, it is his or her job to begin to identify, to articulate, and to motivate others to embrace the collective vision. Teamwork is a crucial piece in the fabric of school life, and the school administrator's role is to promote learning for the myriad of teams found in schools. If each member of an orchestra is an expert musician and shares the same vision for performance, then the important question is whether or not they can actually play together. A team of teachers many have expertise and share a similar vision for the school, but if they cannot work together to help the school attain its goals, then the team will have minimal impact. School administrators need not only have skill in articulating goals but they must learn how to help teams of people judiciously collaborate.

Listed below are key questions for TQE leaders:

- Do I thoroughly understand the implications of our goals?
- How can I most effectively communicate these goals?
- What skills in team learning and group processing do I need to use and model?
- In what ways can I help facilitate this collaboration?

Supplying Individual Support

Before people can effectively work together, they must develop a sense of trust. By administrators' showing genuine respect for staff and concern for their personal feelings, a bond of trust will be formed. Individualized support will take many forms, but to encourage risk taking, administrators need to provide safety nets.

Conflict and change result in tension. Senge (1990) believes the juxtaposition of what we want and where we are relative to what we want generates a "creative tension." School administrators need to keep a careful eye on this tension so that it stretches, but does not explode. Careful attention to the needs of individuals in the school community will ensure that a safety net is available for people as they take risks.

Key questions for TQE leaders are

- What is my relationship with each staff member?
- Is it a formal relationship? Cautious? Sharing? Open?
- What have I done to move that relationship toward one of mutual collaboration?

Providing Intellectual Stimulation

Total quality leaders will challenge staff members to question assumptions about their work and how to discover better ways to solve problems. The school administrator must help staff to fill the gaps between their espoused theory (views they profess) and their theories in use (the theories behind their action). As discussed in chapter 3, there are many school practices (e.g., tracking) that demonstrate the discrepancies between our espoused theories and our actual practices. School leaders will challenge staff members (in nonthreatening ways) by asking them if they truly value their espoused theories. They will find out if staff members are committed to the vision they have collectively formed.

Key questions for TQE leaders are the following:

- In what ways have I challenged my colleagues to keep their paradigms current?
- Do my colleagues' espoused theories and theories in use match?

Holding High-Performance Expectations

There is considerable evidence of the detrimental role that low expectations play in school achievement, particularly for those students from some racial and cultural groups such as African Americans, Native Americans, Puerto Ricans, and Mexican Americans. In their modeling, school leaders must demonstrate high expectations for all students and staff members. In some cases the lowering of expectations is unintentional, thus school leaders through team learning need to strengthen reflection skills; however, no matter how much we reflect on our behaviors, all individuals have blind spots. If we have developed and nurtured trust among our colleagues, then they can help us to see the gaps between our espoused theories and actual practices.

Key questions for TQE leaders are the following:

- In what ways do I convey my performance expectations?

- Do I hold different expectations for people because of their gender? Age? Cultural group?

Cultural Diversity: A Jalapeño in a Candy Jar

In a study of successful Mexican American students, one of the authors interviewed a high school student who said she felt "like a jalapeño in a candy jar." This young woman was referring to being one of the few Hispanic females in a large urban high school. She commented that a jalapeño was just as flavorful as a jelly bean, but you had to learn to appreciate its taste if it was unfamiliar to your palate. Similarly, school personnel need to understand and celebrate all the children in the school community, however foreign their customs, mores, and beliefs.

For many school communities this will require major changes in the school's culture. If school administrators are to facilitate these changes, the challenges are considerable and will require new learning and new skills. To change schools, school administrators must first change themselves. We hope that this book has offered ideas for beginning the change process.

Key Terms and Concepts

School culture. The values, beliefs, and traditions of a school including the underlying social meanings that shape behavior and beliefs.

References

Bennis, W. (1990). *Why leaders can't lead*. San Francisco: Jossey-Bass.
Pascal, R. T. (1990). *Managing on the edge: How the smartest companies use conflict to stay ahead*. New York: Simon & Schuster.
Senge, P. (1990). *The fifth discipline*. New York: Doubleday.

Planning and Troubleshooting Guide

Multiculturalism and TQE
Addressing Cultural Diversity in Schools

Paula A. Cordeiro, Timothy G. Reagan, Linda P. Martinez
University of Connecticut

Enormous changes have taken place in American schools during the past 30 years. Racial and ethnic diversity has never been so great; the U.S. now has the largest number of immigrants in history. The pervasiveness of gender inequality has only lately been widely recognized both in our schools and society at large. Perhaps most dramatic of all, the structure of the American family is different in ways undreamed of just a few years ago.

These changes have greatly complicated our ability to provide an equitable and high-quality learning experience for all students. Yet these are challenges that offer their own unique opportunities. In diversity, there is strength.

In *Multiculturalism and TQE*, Cordeiro, Reagan, and Martinez present *Total Quality Education* (TQE), as the framework for addressing the multiple challenges of student diversity. To develop a multicultural attitude in schools, fundamental shifts must take place in our patterns of thinking and in the ways we respond to differences.

The authors show how to recognize and eliminate the individual and institutional barriers of prejudice and discrimination. They demonstrate that administrators must play a key role in affirming diversity through staff and curriculum development, and by cultivating the involvement of families and communities. To help in the process, specific activities and approaches to broaden awareness, understanding, and communication are provided.

ISBN 0-8039-6107-3 (Paperback only)

CORWIN PRESS, INC.
A Sage Publications Company
2455 Teller Road
Thousand Oaks, CA 91320-2218
Call: 805-499-9774 Fax: 805-499-0871